THE U.S. ARMY INFANTRYMAN

POCKET MANUAL 1941–45

ETO & MTO

Edited by Chris McNab

CASEMATE

Philadelphia & Oxford

Published in the United States of America and
Great Britain in 2021 by
CASEMATE PUBLISHERS
1950 Lawrence Road, Havertown, PA 19083, USA
The Old Music Hall, 106–108 Cowley Road, Oxford OX4 1JE, UK

Introduction and chapter introductory texts by Chris McNab
© Casemate Publishers 2021

Hardback Edition: ISBN 978-1-63624-028-2
Digital Edition: ISBN 978-1-63624-029-9

A CIP record for this book is available from the British Library

Printed and bound in India by Replika Press Pvt. Ltd.

Typeset by Lapiz Digital Services.

For a complete list of Casemate titles, please contact:

CASEMATE PUBLISHERS (US)
Telephone (610) 853-9131
Fax (610) 853-9146
Email: casemate@casematepublishers.com
www.casematepublishers.com

CASEMATE PUBLISHERS (UK)
Telephone (01865) 241249
Fax (01865) 794449
Email: casemate-uk@casematepublishers.co.uk
www.casematepublishers.co.uk

CONTENTS

INTRODUCTION

In August and September 1941, a fictitious war was fought in the state of Louisiana. Some 400,000 U.S. Army troops, a total of 19 divisions, were separated into opposing sides—the Red Army and the Blue Army—and conducted a vast war game over an expanse of 3,400 square miles. Although ultimately an exercise, the "Louisiana Maneuvers" were conducted with deadly seriousness and heavy scrutiny. For by the summer of 1941, it looked increasingly likely that the United States would be drawn into the war in Europe, the U.S. orbit around that conflict becoming ever tighter and faster. Indeed, the exercise was implicitly focused on developing and testing the capabilities required to defeat German *blitzkrieg* tactics.

While the Louisiana Maneuvers were a true combined-arms exercise, the bulk of their combat volume was made up of the U.S. Army infantry. They were in many ways the most basic element of the U.S. military. Their weapons were generally the least powerful of all the major combat branches—mainly small arms, light support weapons and mortars, and hand-operated explosives—with the more powerful firepower coming from supporting armor, artillery, and close-air support (CAS). The American infantryman still relied heavily on his own two feet to move from one place to another, even in the wartime U.S. Army, which was heavily motorized. In action, his job was to get up close to the enemy and take and hold terrain from him, a job that no other branch of service could perform. If the world was going to be freed from Axis occupation, it would ultimately fall to the infantryman to do it.

The United States entered World War II on December 8, 1941, provoked ultimately not by Germany but by the Japanese attack on Pearl Harbor the day before, although Hitler hubristically declared war on the United States on December 11. We should note that just two years before, the strength of the U.S. Army was just 189,839 personnel, making it far smaller than many of the European combatant armies. As the threat of war dawned, therefore, the priority for the U.S. military was to scale up fast, re-arm, and retrain for modern warfare. In 1940, President Franklin D. Roosevelt signed the Selective Training and Service Act, which registered more than 16 million men as eligible for military service. A lottery draft began on October 29, 1940, and by March 1941, 300,000 men had joined regular, reserve, and National Guard Army formations. The numbers grew ever larger month on month, and were naturally galvanized by the onset of war. By 1942, 3.36 million men had been drafted, and by war's end in 1945, a total of 7.42 million soldiers had served in the U.S. Army.

The largest proportion of these personnel would serve in the Mediterranean Theater of Operations (MTO) and European Theater of Operations (ETO)— three million U.S. Army troops were sent to the ETO alone. Army formations were deployed in strength to the Pacific Theater of Operations (PTO), where they fought punishing and costly campaigns, island-hopping alongside the Marines and fighting major overland campaigns in the Philippines. But here we shall focus primarily on the MTO and ETO, mainly to give the book a greater clarity of focus, as the conditions of both service and combat in the PTO were so profoundly different to those of Europe and North Africa.

From late 1942, the U.S. infantry would always be at the tip of the spear in the fight against Hitler's Wehrmacht. The Americans' first taste of major land warfare in the MTO (although not in the PTO) came in November 1942, with the Operation *Torch* landings along the coastline of Morocco and Algiers, before the U.S. forces turned east to squeeze German and Italian forces into and ultimately out of Tunisia. The early American experience of meeting the veteran Germans, expertly led by Generalfeldmarschall Erwin Rommel, was a sobering one. At the Kasserine Pass in Tunisia in February 1943, the U.S. forces suffered a stinging defeat under a German counteroffensive, one that drove them out of their defensive positions and pushed them back west by a distance of some 50 miles before the German juggernaut was finally arrested. The battle cost the U.S. forces 3,300 dead and wounded, many of them "green" infantry who were psychologically unprepared for the sheer shock of battle against an enemy who was, at that stage of the war, simply far more capable than they were. Furthermore, the U.S. Army was still at this time adjusting to the new world of maneuver warfare tactics, which emphasized the coordination, via wireless radio, of infantry, armor, artillery, and aviation into a functional whole capable of maintaining a high tempo of operations. The German armed forces had been embedding these principles since the 1930s, and it would take some time before the Americans caught up.

Still, Kasserine Pass usefully dispelled any patronizing or complacent notions about the enemy, and from this point on the U.S. Army quickly began to improve its game, tactically and operationally. Soon on a man-for-man basis, the U.S. infantry became every bit a match for the Germans they faced, plus the herculean industrial might of the United States would ultimately give U.S. ground forces unrivalled levels of firepower. But there would be no shortcuts in this war, and three long years of campaigning lay ahead of U.S. forces, each new deployment and theater bringing its own set of challenges while inexorably adding to the casualty lists. The U.S. North African campaign lasted until May 1943, a battle in which the U.S. soldiers also had to learn the stark procedures of managing heat, dust, and disease in a tropical climate. (Even later in the climatically more benign ETO, the U.S. Army would suffer about 4.5 non-battle casualties for every individual soldier killed or wounded on the battlefield.) From North Africa, it was then on to Sicily in July 1943, Operation *Husky* being one of the largest amphibious landings in history. It took a month of heavy fighting and more than 10,000 U.S. casualties to clear the island, then the following September the Allied forces stepped across the Straits of Messina to invade mainland Italy. Fighting in Italy would last until the end of the war, and despite Churchill's early suggestion of Italy being the "soft underbelly" of Europe the fighting there was of exceptional ferocity. The U.S. infantry in Italy spent months of grinding action attempting to dislodge German forces from a series of obdurate defensive lines, etched with imagination into mountains and along rivers.

On June 6, 1944, the Allies finally began the liberation of occupied Europe with the vast amphibious landings on the beaches of Normandy, the opening acts of Operation *Overlord*. The landings themselves brought a salutary indication of the cost the U.S. infantry would pay to help free Europe: the 1st and 29th Infantry Divisions alongside U.S. Army Rangers took 2,400 casualties just getting ashore on Omaha Beach. Nevertheless, the beachheads were secured, and eventually 13 U.S. Army infantry divisions would be committed to the fighting in Normandy, which rivaled World War I in terms of casualty rates. Eventually the Allies inched their way out into France and wider occupied Europe, moving through Belgium, Luxembourg, the Netherlands, and into Germany itself.

Compared to the vastness of the PTO, the ETO was a relatively small theater. Like the PTO, however, the levels of resistance to the Allied advance were prosecuted with absolute commitment. Places the typical U.S. infantryman had never even heard of became the location for events that, if they survived, would become the defining experiences of their lives. The battle of the Hürtgen Forest, fought from September to December 1944, is a case in point. This area of dark and ancient forest, 54 square miles in extent and lying in Germany just east of the German–Belgian border, soaked up the bloody efforts of 11 U.S. infantry divisions and two Ranger battalions (plus many armored and artillery formations) as the Americans attempted to clear the forest of a German defensive force who had their jaws set firm. The nature of the terrain reduced the effectiveness of American heavy firepower, so it was largely left to the infantry to wrestle each position out of German hands, with fighting often taking place hand-to-hand. By the time the forest was eventually in American hands, the U.S. First Army had taken up to 55,000 casualties, compared to c. 28,000 on the German side. Compounding the agonies for U.S. infantry, shortly thereafter Hitler launched his powerful counteroffensive in the Ardennes, which for a time saw many frontline U.S. infantry units nearly wiped out or surrounded.

To arrest this last gasp of the Third Reich on the Western Front cost an additional 89,000 U.S. casualties. Yet by February 1945, it was clear that German resistance was finally tottering, culminating in the German surrender in May. While the U.S. infantry in Europe licked their wounds, the U.S. infantry in the Pacific nonetheless kept fighting for another four months, at hideous cost. Some 4,675 U.S. Army troops alone were killed during the battle of Okinawa (March 26–July 2,

1945), part of a total of 50,000 U.S. casualties. There were an additional 63,000 U.S. casualties in the effort to the clear the Philippines.

The General George S. Patton, commander of the U.S. Seventh Army, who spent 36 years of his life in the service of the U.S. Army, once said "I am a soldier, I fight where I am told, and I win where I fight." This characteristically punchy and blunt statement of Patton could be applied *en masse* to the U.S. Army infantrymen of World War II. Hundreds of thousands of young men, the majority of whom had never set out with life plans to join the armed forces, were drafted, put in uniform, trained, and sent across the globe to fight one of the most capable professional armies in history. Yet they rose to the challenge. By the end of the war, the U.S. Army infantry was an efficient, aggressive, well-equipped, and battle-proven force. They took on a peer adversary and won, and in so doing were essential to the liberation of a continent from German control.

This book, through a collection of primary sources, opens a window into both the doctrine and the experience of the U.S. Army infantryman in World War II. These sources take U.S. on the infantryman's journey from training and deployment through to frontline combat, and from the immediate pre-war years to the very end of the conflict. Uniting them all is a sense of the U.S. military engaged in a process of education regarding modern warfare, adjusting theory and acquiring hard-won lessons as it fine-tuned its operational capabilities. This process was critical not just to winning battles and delivering campaigns, but was also fundamental to raising the chances of the individual soldier making it alive to the end of the war. Particularly in the final chapter, where we focus on "lessons learned" documents, we see how important it was to push combat knowledge down the chain of command until it reached company and platoon commanders, noncommissioned officers (NCOs), and the regular infantryman. Although every infantry soldier knew that mortality could be capricious and arbitrary in wartime, knowledge acquired through either information or experience could be the deciding factor in surviving the day.

CHAPTER I

ORGANIZATION AND PURPOSE

The largest of the U.S. Army formations in World War II was the army group, composed of a minimum of two armies, each of which consisted of two corps-level formations. In turn, each individual corps was formed from a minimum of two divisions. An individual infantry division was, from 1940, organized in a "triangular" arrangement of three infantry regiments, each of these regiments consisting of a headquarters company, three infantry battalions, and cannon, antitank, and service companies. In total, the division had a total complement (1943–44) of 14,255 officers and men, with 9,354 of those soldiers in the infantry battalions.

The field manual FM 7-20, *Infantry Battalion*, orientates the soldier to the composition and organization of the battalion, the unit to which the infantryman would have the closest sense of higher-level affiliation. The list of battalion staff duties is particularly useful for breaking down the way in which an infantry battalion functioned, from collecting intelligence to organizing transport and medical services. Elsewhere, the manual notes that "Aggressiveness and the ability to take prompt and decisive action are prime requisites for a successful battalion commander. By these qualities he inspires confidence. By his boldness, energy, and initiative he influences both individual and collective conduct and performance." This trickle-down view of morale was indeed crucial to the capabilities of an infantry battalion, and while our book here is primarily focused on junior officers and enlisted men, we should always acknowledge the heavy burden of expectations placed on those further up the command tree.

From FM 7-20, *Infantry Battalion* **(1944)**

CHAPTER 1
GENERAL

1. ROLE OF THE INFANTRY BATTALION. The battalion is the basic tactical unit of Infantry. It usually operates as an element of the infantry regiment. Its mission is assigned by the regimental commander, and its actions are coordinated with those of other units of the regiment. Exceptionally, the battalion may be detached from the regiment to perform an independent mission. It has administrative functions.

2. COMPOSITION. The battalion consists of a headquarters and headquarters company, three rifle companies, and a heavy weapons company. Medical personnel and nonorganic transportation are attached.

   a. Battalion headquarters and headquarters company.

   (1) The headquarters consists of the battalion commander (a lieutenant colonel) and certain members of his staff.

   (2) The headquarters company consists of company headquarters; a battalion headquarters section; a communication platoon; an ammunition and pioneer platoon; and an antitank platoon.

[…]

   b. Rifle company. Each rifle company consists of a company headquarters, three rifle platoons, and a weapons platoon.

   c. Heavy weapons company. The heavy weapons company consists of a company headquarters, two caliber .30 (heavy) machine-gun platoons, and an 81-mm mortar platoon.

   d. Attachments. For operations, the battalion section from the regimental medical detachment joins its battalion.

   e. Motor transport.

   (1) Organic motor transport of the infantry battalion consists only of the company transport of its component elements.

   (2) The battalion trains are an integral part of the regimental trains. They include kitchen and baggage, ammunition, and maintenance vehicles organically assigned to the service company, and medical vehicles organically assigned to the medical detachment. In operations, and when the battalion supply echelon is operative, the battalion section of the service company transportation platoon (regimental trains) joins its battalion, except for those elements which may be retained under regimental control.

[…]

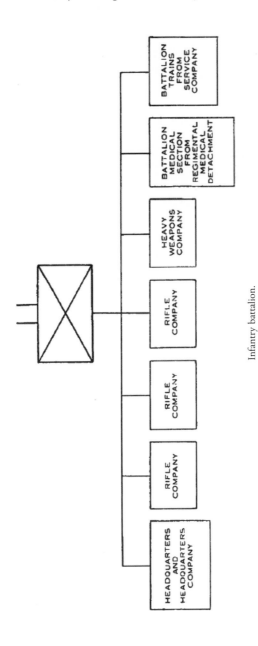

Infantry battalion.

CHAPTER 2

SECTION II
BATTALION STAFF AND STAFF DUTIES

7. COMPOSITION. *a.* The battalion unit staff consists of the following:

    (1) Executive officer (second-in-command).

    (2) Adjutant (S-1) (company commander, battalion headquarters company).

    (3) Intelligence officer (S-2).

    (4) Operations and training officer (S-3).

    (5) Supply officer (S-4) (from the service company).

b. Certain officers who are charged with technical and administrative duties, and who are commanders of subordinate, attached, or supporting units, have staff duties as advisers to the battalion commander and staff in matters pertaining to their specialties in addition to their primary duties of command. Such officers are—

    (1) Battalion motor transport officer (second-in-command, battalion headquarters company).

    (2) Company commander of the heavy weapons company.

    (3) Antitank officer (commanding battalion antitank platoon).

    (4) Communication officer (commanding battalion communication platoon).

    (5) Platoon leader of the battalion ammunition and pioneer

    platoon (battalion munitions and gas officer).

    (6) Surgeon (commanding the battalion medical section).

    (7) Commanders of attached units, such as regimental cannon, artillery, tank, antitank, engineer, or chemical units.

    (8) Artillery liaison officer (from an artillery battalion in direct support).

    (9) Liaison officer from adjacent units.

8. ORGANIZATION OF BATTALION HEADQUARTERS FOR COMBAT. The battalion command group should be so organized that it can function continuously, day and night, throughout an operation. To this end, staff officers are trained to perform the duties of other staff officers. Each staff officer keeps brief notes to enable him to inform the commander, or other staff officer, of the situation.

9. EXECUTIVE OFFICER. *a.* The executive officer is second-in-command and principal assistant of the battalion commander. He performs such duties as are delegated to him by the latter.

b. The executive officer usually remains at the command post when the battalion commander is away. He makes decisions in the name of the latter as the occasion demands. He keeps abreast of the situation and of the battalion commander's plans, and keeps the battalion commander informed of the strength, morale, training, equipment, supply, and tactical situation of the battalion. He coordinates all staff activities. He verifies the execution of orders and notifies the battalion commander of any matters needing correction. He supervises the keeping of the unit situation map and checks reports and orders prepared by the staff for correctness, completeness, clarity, and brevity.

10. S-1. *a.* The company commander of battalion headquarters company is also the battalion adjutant, S-1.

b. The duties of S-1 include—

(1) Receiving and delivering replacements to units.

(2) Securing means for recreation and for building and maintaining morale.

(3) Submitting recommendations for decorations, citations, honors, and awards as required.

(4) Maintaining strength and casualty reports.

(5) Maintaining the unit journal.

(6) Selecting the exact location of the command post when so directed, in conjunction with the communication officer.

(7) Arranging the interior installations (except signal communication agencies) and supervising the movements of the command post.

(8) Allotting space to subordinate units in bivouac and assembly areas (coordinating with S-3).

(9) Arranging for quartering parties. The battalion S-l, if available, will accompany quartering parties; otherwise he will arrange for the detail of another officer.

(10) Preparing data for tactical reports.

(11) Organizing the defense of the command post.

(12) Supervising mail distribution and collection.

11. S-2. *a.* The battalion intelligence officer (S-2) is primarily concerned with the collection, recording, evaluation, and dissemination of information of the enemy and enemy-held terrain, and with counterintelligence measures. He must be prepared at any time to give his commander a synopsis of the hostile situation and an estimate of the enemy capabilities as they affect the battalion.

b. The duties of S-2 include—

(1) Planning of reconnaissances, and coordinating with S-3 the security measures relating to patrols and observation posts; personally making reconnaissances when the nature of the information desired indicates the necessity for such action.

(2) Insuring that S-2 data are posted on the unit situation map.

(3) Preparing data for tactical reports.

(4) Giving special training to the battalion intelligence personnel and controlling them during operations.

(5) Preparing intelligence plans and orders.

(6) Establishing and supervising the operation of battalion observation posts.

(7) Coordinating battalion information-collecting agencies. Exchanging information with the regiment and with adjacent and subordinate units.

(8) Coordinating with prisoner of war interrogation teams; in their absence, examining and promptly forwarding to the regiment captured personnel, documents, and materiel.

(9) Procuring maps, aerial photographs, and photomaps from regimental S-2 and distributing them.

(10) Verifying camouflage and concealment measures.

(11) Coordinating counterintelligence measures in the battalion, including censorship.

12. S-3. *a.* The battalion operations and training officer (S-3) is concerned primarily with the training and tactical operations of the battalion. He must be prepared at any time to give the battalion commander a synopsis of the situation of the battalion and of adjacent and supporting troops, and to recommend possible lines of action.

b. The duties of S-3 include—

(1) Planning of security measures, and coordinating measures for reconnaissance with S-2.

(2) Insuring that S-3 data are posted on the unit situation map.

(3) Preparing data for tactical reports.

(4) Planning and supervising all training in accordance with the regimental training program.

(5) Maintaining training records and preparing training reports.

(6) Selecting initial and subsequent general locations of the command post (coordinating with the communication officer), if not previously designated by the regiment.

(7) Making terrain analyses.

(8) Preparing detailed plans based upon the battalion commander's decision (coordinating with S-1 and S-4).

(9) Preparing operation maps and overlays.

(10) Assisting the battalion commander in the preparation of field orders (coordinating with other staff officers).

(11) Supervising signal communication and liaison with higher, adjacent, and subordinate units.

(12) Transmitting orders and instructions for the battalion commander.

13. S-4. *a.* The battalion supply officer (S-4) is assigned to the transportation platoon, service company. He performs staff and supply duties as directed by the battalion commander and is responsible for the functioning of the battalion supply system in the field and in combat, with particular reference to rations, water, ammunition, gasoline, and oil.

b. The duties of S-4 include—

(1) Preparing the battalion supply plan based upon the regimental supply plan and the tactical plan of the battalion commander.

(2) Controlling elements of the company transport and battalion trains (ammunition and kitchen and baggage trains) when they are operating under battalion control. He is assisted in this duty by the battalion motor transport officer.

(3) Coordinating with the regimental supply echelon for details relating to the movement of battalion supplies and trains.

(4) Ascertaining the supply requirements of companies and attached units through personal contact.

(5) Establishing and operating the battalion ammunition supply point, and procuring ammunition from the regimental ammunition supply point. He is assisted in this duty by the battalion munitions officer (platoon leader of the ammunition and pioneer platoon).

(6) Insuring, during combat, that an adequate supply of ammunition is delivered to companies, the antitank platoon, and any attached units.

(7) Making a reconnaissance for covered routes between the battalion and the regimental supply points and points of release of trains, and regulating the movement of vehicles on these routes.

(8) Keeping in close touch with the battalion command post in order to coordinate supply operations with the tactical situation, and supply plans with the tactical plans of the battalion commander.

(9) Planning and conducting the defense of the battalion ammunition supply point and of transportation under battalion control.

14. MOTOR TRANSPORT OFFICER. *a.* The motor transport officer is second-in-command of the battalion headquarters company. His staff duties as motor transport officer constitute his principal functions.

b. The duties of the motor transport officer include—

(1) In march or approach march situations, controlling such company transport and elements of the regimental trains as may be grouped under battalion control.

(2) Supervising, coordinating, and expediting the movement of company weapon carriers, ammunition train vehicles, and hand-carrying parties within the battalion area (between company areas and the battalion ammunition supply point) so as to insure an adequate supply of ammunition to all companies.

(3) Supervising and coordinating the activities of second echelon motor maintenance facilities operating within the battalion.

15. HEAVY WEAPONS COMPANY COMMANDER. The heavy weapons company commander, in addition to his command duties, assists the battalion commander in developing the battalion fire plan. He accompanies the battalion commander on reconnaissance, or makes separate reconnaissance and recommendations for the employment of supporting heavy weapons as directed.

16. ANTITANK OFFICER. The leader of the battalion antitank platoon is the battalion antitank officer, and assists the battalion commander in the planning and execution of the battalion antitank defense. He accompanies the battalion commander on reconnaissance or makes a separate reconnaissance and recommendations for the employment and coordination of antitank means as directed.

17. COMMUNICATION OFFICER. *a.* The battalion communication officer is responsible for the technical training and proficiency of the communication platoon of the battalion headquarters company, and for supervision of such technical training of communication personnel throughout the battalion as may be delegated to him by the battalion commander. He is responsible to the battalion commander for the planning, installation, operation, and maintenance of the battalion communication system. His duties include recommending (usually to S-3) initial and subsequent locations of the command post, if not previously designated by the regiment.

[...]

18. PLATOON LEADER OF AMMUNITION AND PIONEER PLATOON. *a.* The leader of the battalion ammunition and pioneer platoon performs such staff duties as the battalion commander may direct. He is charged with the training and supervision of his platoon in the execution of their ammunition, supply, and pioneer tasks. He accomplishes simple field engineering (pioneer) tasks not requiring the technical and special equipment of engineer troops. He assigns duties to members of his platoon in accordance with the requirements of the situation after consultation with the battalion S-4. He is also that battalion gas officer and battalion munitions officer.

b. His duties include—

(1) Performing pioneer reconnaissances; controlling the pioneer operations of his platoon.

(2) Assisting S-4 in selecting, establishing, and operating the battalion ammunition supply point.

(3) Within the battalion, supervising and coordinating gas defense training, gas defense measures, and use of decontaminating agents.

(4) Inspecting gas defense equipment.

(5) Supervising gas reconnaissance of routes and areas before their use by troops.

(6) Supervising the activities of his platoon in the employment, detection, and removal of mines and booby traps.

19. SURGEON. *a.* The battalion surgeon is a member of the battalion commander's staff and commands the battalion medical section. His staff functions pertain to the health and medical service of the battalion. He is the battalion sanitary inspector. He supervises the technical instruction of the battalion in personal hygiene, field sanitation, first aid, and malaria control. The battalion section normally has no administrative or supply functions. The battalion surgeon, when practicable, is present when field orders are issued.

b. His duties include—

(1) Obtaining from the battalion commander available information of tactical plans for the battalion; making a medical estimate of the situation; reconnoitering for aid station sites; submitting medical plans (usually through S-4) to the battalion commander for approval.

(2) Establishing the aid station, supervising its operation and personally assisting in the care and treatment of casualties.

(3) Evacuating sick and wounded within the battalion area to the battalion aid station.

(4) Keeping the battalion commander, the regimental surgeon, and the collecting company in immediate support informed of the situation as to sick and wounded.

(5) Making timely requests to the regimental surgeon for special support, additional supplies, additional personnel, and emergency evacuation of casualties.

20. COMMANDERS OF ATTACHED UNITS. *a.* Commanders of attached units are advisers to the battalion commander and staff.

b. Their duties include—

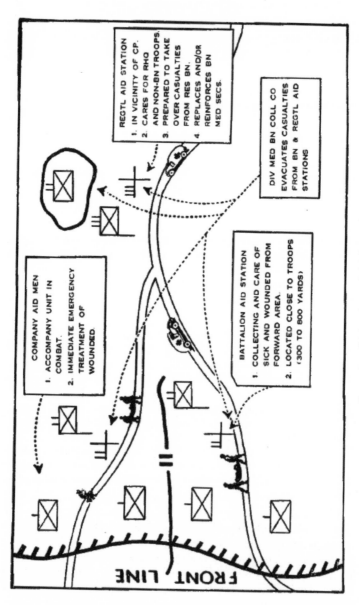

Evacuation of sick and wounded (schematic).

(1) Submitting plans and recommendations to the battalion commander and staff for the tactical employment of their units.

(2) Maintaining communication with the battalion commander, and keeping him advised of the combat capabilities of their units.

21. ARTILLERY LIAISON OFFICER AND FORWARD OBSERVERS. *a.* An artillery unit in direct support of an infantry unit sends a liaison officer to each supported battalion. The liaison officer is the personal representative of the artillery commander and remains under his command. He contacts the infantry battalion commander in time to accompany the latter on reconnaissance and secure detailed information as to specific fire missions desired, and thereafter remains with him. Artillery employs both wire and radio for communication; in emergencies, the infantry battalion commander should make his wire net available for artillery fire direction.

b. The primary mission of the artillery liaison officer is to advise and assist the infantry battalion commander in obtaining the desired supporting or reinforcing fires, and to keep his own commander informed of the situation. He must be able to inform the infantry battalion commander of the capabilities of the artillery in delivering any fires desired, and to transmit promptly to the artillery commander requests for supporting fires. To enable the liaison officer to carry out his mission, the infantry battalion commander must keep him informed at all times of the location of hostile and friendly units, the plan of maneuver, the plan of fires, and the immediate needs of the battalion.

c. As a secondary mission, the liaison officer adjusts the fires of his unit when necessary.

d. Direct-support field artillery battalions, and, in most cases, battalions reinforcing the fires of direct-support battalions, send out forward observers, usually in the ratio of one to each front-line company or similar unit. Forward observers are controlled and coordinated by the artillery liaison officer with the infantry battalion. All artillery observers coming forward to observe in an infantry battalion zone or sector report to the artillery liaison officer with that battalion in order to insure properly coordinated employment of all observers and to exploit all means of observation. Forward observers also keep in close contact with the forward elements of the infantry battalion.

e. The forward observer has two general missions. His primary mission is to observe and adjust artillery fire on those hostile elements which interfere with the mission of the unit with which he is working. His secondary mission is to keep the artillery battalion informed of the situation. The forward observer is not attached to the supported unit. He is not restricted to the zone of action or defense area of the supported unit. He goes where he can obtain the observation necessary to give effective artillery support.

22. CANNON COMPANY REPRESENTATIVES. Cannon platoons are frequently utilized for furnishing close supporting fires for front-line battalions. One or more platoons may support the action of the regiment as a whole. When supporting or attached to a leading or front-line battalion, the platoon leader reports directly to the battalion commander. When practicable, the platoon leader accompanies the battalion commander on reconnaissance; thereafter, he remains with or leaves his own representative with the battalion commander. The platoon leader seeks detailed information as to specific fire missions desired; the majority of these will be fire upon targets of opportunity. Frequent displacement of weapons is required in order that they may not be engaged by hostile artillery. Communication is maintained between the platoon leader and his sections by means of voice radios, sound-powered telephones, messengers, and arm-and-hand signals; pyrotechnics also may be used.

23. LIAISON OFFICERS. *a.* Staff or other officers may be used as liaison officers. They may be sent to higher or subordinate units or to adjacent units (including advanced reconnaissance elements under control of higher commanders). Such missions will usually involve brief visits to other units and prompt return to the battalion commander, in order that they may be readily available for subsequent missions.

b. Prior to departure on a mission, a liaison officer should receive from the battalion commander—

(1) Definite and detailed instructions, in writing if practicable, as to the liaison mission.

(2) Information of the battalion commander's plans, particularly if they affect the unit to which he is to be sent.

(3) Information as to what facilities (signal and transportation) are available for transmission of any messages the liaison officer is to send prior to his return.

c. Prior to departure the liaison officer should also—

(1) Familiarize himself with the situation of his own unit and so far as practicable with that of the unit to which sent.

(2) Insure that arrangements for communication (signal and transportation) are adequate.

(3) Obtain credentials in writing unless obviously unnecessary.

d. On arrival at the headquarters to which sent, the liaison officer should—

(1) Report promptly to the commander, stating his mission and exhibiting his directive or credentials, if in writing.

(2) Arrange for the transmission of messages he may be required to send.

(3) Familiarize himself with the situation of the unit to which sent.

(4) Accomplish his mission without interfering with the operations of the headquarters to which sent.

(5) Keep a record of messages sent to the battalion commander.

(6) Advise the visited unit commander of the contents of messages to be sent to his battalion commander.

(7) Make prompt report to his battalion commander if he is unable to accomplish his liaison mission.

(8) Report his departure to the visited unit commander on the completion of his mission.

e. On return to his battalion commander the liaison officer should—

(1) Report on his mission.

(2) Transmit promptly any requests of the commander from whose headquarters he has just returned.

In the following passages from FM 7-5, *Organization and Tactics of Infantry: The Rifle Battalion* (1940), the authors emphasize the "moral qualities" of the infantry soldier and his leaders. This section should not be regarded as a preamble to the meat of the extract, in which the composition of the infantry unit is described, as the infantry during World War II had to draw deeply from the wells of resilience and courage. Infantry deployments during the conflict could be profoundly long, compounding the demands of frontline life with those of homesickness. The U.S. 1st Infantry Division, for example, was deployed on frontline combat duties for 442 days during the war; it was common for an individual soldier in the ETO not to see the United States for a period of about 11 months. Casualties would also change the personnel of a platoon, company, or battalion with voracious appetite— in the Normandy campaign casualty levels ran at 100–200 percent of establishment strength. Having leaders and personalities who could hold the unit together during such uniquely hostile circumstances was imperative.

**From FM 7-5, *Organization and Tactics of Infantry:
The Rifle Battalion* (1940)**

PART ONE
INFANTRY CHARACTERISTICS AND ORGANIZATION

CHAPTER 1
MORAL QUALITIES, LEADERSHIP, AND TRAINING

SECTION I
THE INFANTRY SOLDIER

1. DECISIVE ELEMENT IN WAR.—Man is the final and decisive element in war. Combat is a moral struggle, and victory goes to the side which refuses to become discouraged. Numerical factors, armament, equipment, and technical training affect morale but at the same time derive their full value from the moral qualities of the soldier.

2. MAIN OBJECTIVE OF TRAINING.—The main task in the making of a soldier is to inculcate ideals of military conduct which permit military technique to be utilized effectively. In general the ideals of the individual will be the military standards inculcated in and accepted by his unit.

3. MORALE.—Morale is affected by many influences. In large part it rests upon the soldier's confidence in himself, his comrades, and his leaders. To build and sustain the spirit of comradeship is the leader's greatest task. The soldier must be taught to accept responsibility for the welfare and the actions of his team mates. He must feel that the record of his organization is his record. He must avoid any act or word that may spread despondency. He must refuse to be disheartened by hardships or reverses. Often his best contribution to victory will be the encouragement of others.

4. DISCIPLINE.—*a.* The soldier is disciplined when he has learned to place the mission of his unit above his personal welfare and to conform his action to the will of the leader. Discipline carries with it the spirit of teamwork and mutual trust.

b. Response to leadership.—The soldier gives his entire loyalty to his leader in return for loyalty to him and his comrades. In battle his attitude is modeled on that of his leaders. In peace he adopts the standards of military conduct held up by leaders whom he respects and admires.

c. Citizenship training.—Soldierly ideals are the more easily acquired if the ideals of the individual's civil environment provide a suitable basis. The task of making soldiers will be more difficult when considerable citizenship training is required. Organizational unity is much easier to attain where a strong faith in national institutions underlies the soldier's loyalty to his leader and his unit.

SECTION II
THE GROUP AND UNIT

5. COHESION.—*a.* Men are grouped primarily with a view to their training for and use in combat. The combat group acquires cohesion through common experience. Individuals constantly trained, quartered, and fed together develop a feeling of solidarity. Drill, if held to simple, precise movements for short periods, rapidly develops group feeling. The soldier identifies himself with the group, gives it his allegiance, and conforms to its standards.

b. The time required to develop military group cohesion depends on many factors, such as the ability of the leaders, the methods of training, and the ideals brought from civil life by individuals. A military organization emerges only when a cohesive group united by common military ideals, confident in its skill in arms, has been developed. Individual skill with weapons alone will not give a group the cohesion necessary to fill the role of Infantry in battle. Infantry units fight in small, isolated groups, often removed from the direct influence of officers, and derive their cohesion from the unity inculcated by association and training. The time required to develop a cohesive military group exceeds the period needed to train the individual in the various military skills.

6. ESPRIT DE CORPS.—*a. General*—(1) Every effort is made to develop the pride of individuals in their group. Commendation and especial privileges promptly awarded for group excellence stimulate unit esprit. Individuals may be criticized or punished for falling below the group standard, but group penalties separate the leader from his group and destroy cohesion. The public opinion of the group is the most powerful lever of discipline and the most effective means of bringing about conformity with military standards.

(2) The soldier gives his allegiance in varying degree to different groups. The company is usually the unit which inculcates group ideals of conduct. Higher units derive their moral unity chiefly through the cohesion of the officers. The history and battle record of the troops attach chiefly to the regiment which forms the object of the soldier's deepest sentimental devotion and inspiration. Battalion and company solidarity, though essential, should not be developed at the expense of regimental group feeling. Occasional resort to competition has value for the purpose of stimulating interest, but systematic competition between companies tends to break the regiment into jealous groups and impairs its teamwork.

(3) So far as practicable, platoons and squads should be kept intact and given the greatest possible degree of permanence. They are elementary tactical teams which are held together in battle by the spirit of comradeship and the direct personal influence of their leaders.

b. Group standards.—The individuals of a unit habitually act in accordance with the military standards which the group has accepted. The proper standards are inculcated by the leader through constant example and suggestion in various ways. Formal instruction as to desirable ideals is of little avail. Violations of accepted group standards must be punished promptly. Repressive measures are, however, only for the few who are not strong enough to observe the standards they recognize as correct or who are inherently inadaptable to military purposes. Such measures are not the bases for the government of units. When esprit de corps is high, condemnation by the public opinion of the group constitutes the main support of discipline.

c. Basis of group unity.—Group ideals are based on national ideals and patriotism. Methods of training and employing soldiers are adapted to the American characteristics of individual initiative, self-reliance, and responsiveness to leadership. American unity is derived from community of ideals. National differences between people of foreign descent rapidly vanish in America. The soldier is instructed in the simple principles of American government and the elements of American history.

[…]

CHAPTER 3
GENERAL ORGANIZATION OF THE INFANTRY

30. GENERAL.—The details of infantry organization, the allotment of weapons, and the distribution of the major items of equipment and transportation are shown in current Tables of Organization. Minor changes resulting from developments in weapons may be expected from time to time.

31. INFANTRY UNITS.—*a. Squad.*—(1) The squad is the elementary combat unit. It is the largest infantry unit habitually controlled by the voice and signals of its leader. A well-trained squad constitutes a team capable of resisting the disintegrating influences of battle and carrying out its assigned mission.

(2) The rifle squad consists of a leader, a second-in-command, and five to ten riflemen.

(3) Personnel armed with weapons heavier than the rifle i.e., the automatic rifle, light machine gun, light mortar, heavy machine gun, caliber .50 machine gun, heavy mortar, and antitank guns—are organized in squads for purposes of control. In general, these squads consist of a squad leader and a gun crew to operate one or more of these weapons.

(4) For purposes of control, weapon squads are equipped with light and heavy machine guns. 60-mm mortars and 37-mm guns are grouped into sections which generally consist of two squads and a section leader.

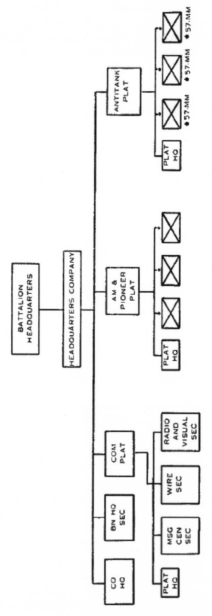

Headquarters and headquarters company, infantry battalion.

b. Rifle platoon.—Rifle and automatic rifle squads are grouped together in the rifle platoon. The platoon is the smallest unit with capacity for deployment in depth and width and endowed with independent power of maneuver. It includes no weapons appreciably less mobile than those of the rifle squad nor any weapons presenting considerable relief in firing position.

c. Company.—The company is the basic infantry unit with administrative and supply functions. It comprises a company headquarters and several platoons with the agencies necessary for their control, subsistence, and administration. Companies are classified as combat companies and headquarters and service companies.

(1) Combat companies of rifle regiments include rifle companies, antitank gun companies, and heavy weapons companies. The rifle company combines the action of several rifle platoons with that of a weapons platoon. It is the smallest unit which habitually organizes a base of fire in attack. It contains only elements which have a normal march mobility approximating that of the rifleman. The light machine gun and the light mortars follow the riflemen by covered approaches; the bursts of speed of the rifleman are not required of them. Heavy weapons companies comprise machine-gun, mortar, and antitank platoons. The antitank gun company comprises three platoons.

(2) Headquarters companies are principally constituted by groups charged with collecting information and disseminating orders and instructions. They may include other elements not large enough to justify a separate supply and administrative overhead.

(3) Service companies furnish staff, supply, and transportation personnel, and operate transportation.

d. Battalion.—The rifle battalion is the basic tactical unit of Infantry. It consists of a headquarters and a headquarters detachment, three rifle companies, and a heavy weapons company. The battalion constitutes a complete infantry unit capable of assignment to a mission requiring the application of all the usual foot Infantry means of action. Organically, it includes no weapon which cannot be manhandled over a distance of several hundred yards.

e. Regiment.—The infantry regiment is the complete tactical and administrative unit. The regimental commander, in addition to coordinating the action of his own units in battle, usually motivates the action of a varying allotment of weapons of supporting arms, particularly artillery.

CHAPTER 2
TRAINING AND DEPLOYMENT

Once the United States was at war, the demands of frontline combat produced a near-insatiable demand for new personnel, both to stock new divisions with manpower and to act as replacements for casualties. To give a sense of the manpower required, note that the War Department activated 38 new divisions in 1942 and 17 divisions in 1943 alone. The training program for a soldier entering a newly activated division broke down as follows from November 1942: 13 weeks of Basic and Individual Training, 11 weeks of Small Unit Training, and 11 weeks of Combined Arms Training, each of the training stages integrating the soldier into larger unit and formation maneuvers. The Basic and Individual Training was the most formative in terms of transforming the raw recruit into a functioning soldier. Roughly dividing the program into phases, the initial month of training focused on imparting basic military knowledge, such as etiquette, discipline, first aid, map reading, and basic tactics, while the second month progressed to physical conditioning, obstacle courses, rifle training, grenade-throwing, bayonet drills. The final month or so would then bind the whole together in squad-level tactical exercises and weapons qualifications.

As the war progressed, the training periods were adjusted slightly to reflect the needs emerging from frontline experience. By April 1943, Basic and Individual Training lasted 14 weeks and each of the two following phases received an additional week. From August 1943 the basic training phase was further increased to 17 weeks, which included four weeks of small-unit training.

In the following passages from FM 7-5, *Organization and Tactics of Infantry: The Rifle Battalion* (1940) and FM 21-20, *Physical Training* (1941), we see some of the basic principles of infantry training as they were established on the approach to war.

From FM 7-5, *Organization and Tactics of Infantry:*
***The Rifle Battalion* (1940)**

CHAPTER 1

SECTION IV
TRAINING DOCTRINES

10. GENERAL.—The fundamental training doctrines are prescribed in FM 100-5, FM 21-5, and in this manual. Special instructions in regard to military training are published in periodical training directives.

11. OFFICERS.—*a. Duties and training.*—The training of officers is continuous throughout their service. Theoretical instruction is accomplished by means of troop schools (AR 350-2600), the various schools of the military educational system (AR 350-5), and by individual application and study. It is the duty of every officer to apply himself to the study of his profession in order to increase his knowledge and proficiency in the duties he may be called upon to perform. It is the duty of every commander to encourage and assist his subordinates in their efforts to increase their professional knowledge and attainments. The practical training of officers is derived from actual experience in command or staff duties appropriate to their grades.

b. Objectives of schools.—Troop schools are important agencies of a unit commander in the training of his unit. The objects are to—

(1) Prepare the personnel of the command to carry out the current training program or prospective operations.

(2) Coordinate and insure uniformity in the training and action of the command.

(3) Provide basic instruction for newly appointed officers.

c. Applicatory exercises.—The principal means of imparting tactical instruction to officers comprise applicatory exercises, such as map problems, terrain exercises, and tactical rides or walks, and field and combat exercises. Command post exercises are valuable for the training of staffs. Leaders and troops are trained in application of combat fundamentals in field exercises and maneuvers.

d. Avoidance of excessive specialization.—Infantry officers should become familiar with the various types of infantry units. This is a responsibility of regimental commanders. Infantry officers likewise must become familiar with the powers and limitations of the associated arms. In particular it is desirable that artillery, armored forces, and aviation be included or represented in battalion or regimental exercises.

e. Training plans.—It is the duty of every commander to make the necessary plans for the training of his command. Commanders of units down to and including battalions prepare and issue programs prescribing the general plan for training the command over an extended period of time. Schedules prescribing detailed instruction for the conduct of training in accordance with the program are issued by commanders of companies and similar units for all training within the unit and by a higher commander for such training as is to be conducted under his personal direction. Schedules are usually issued weekly. They apportion the time available to the several subjects of instruction.

f. Supervision.—Supervision of training is a function of command and is carried out, when practicable, by the unit commander in person. It may consist of daily supervision, training inspections, or tactical inspections. Daily supervision is informal and should not interrupt the continuity of training. Except for cogent reasons, intervention in the work of a subordinate while he is engaged in the training of his unit should be avoided.

12. NONCOMMISSIONED OFFICER.—*a. Role.*—The noncommissioned officers are the leaders and instructors of their units. All basic instruction of enlisted men is given by noncommissioned officers. Observance of this fundamental greatly increases the prestige of group leaders and enhances the discipline of the group.

b. Scope of training.—Sergeants assigned the platoons are trained as platoon leaders. Where practicable in rifle companies, sergeants assigned to rifle platoons are also trained as leaders of mortar and light machine-gun sections. They are instructed in the tactics of composite groupings, such as the rifle platoon, reinforced by a light machine-gun section, acting as an outpost support; advance or rear party or reconnaissance detachment.

c. Schools.—The purpose of schools is to equip noncommissioned officers with the necessary knowledge and skill to lead and instruct their units in an effective manner. They teach the tactical procedure governing the employment of small units and develop the pertinent methods of instruction.

d. Administrative and disciplinary responsibility.—Noncommissioned officers should become accustomed to the exercise of command through the performance of administrative and disciplinary duties as well as the duties of instructors and tactical leaders. Each leader should be taught that his exercise of authority over his unit is complete and extends to all phases of the soldier's life. He should be held to his responsibilities.

13. TRAINING OF INDIVIDUALS.—*a. Physical.*—The physical fitness, endurance, and condition of individual members of a command are among the most important concerns of those responsible for training. Voluntary athletics should be encouraged, and quickening exercises, group games, and mass athletics included in the training program so as to provide a certain amount of athletics for every man in the command. Officers encourage, supervise, and at times participate in the athletics

of their units. A limited participation by officers in competitive games as members of unit teams is permissible as a means of stimulating interest but should not be encouraged as a systematic practice.

b. Development of offensive spirit.—Training is so conducted as to prepare the troops for eventual offensive warfare. Troops are initially grounded in the elements of defensive action in order that they may not only be qualified for emergency defensive missions but also have an understanding of the problem of the individual soldier and the small unit in attack. From the beginning of his training the soldier should be imbued with the spirit of individual aggressive action.

c. Combat instructions.—The combat instruction of the individual soldier and group begins at an early period of the soldier's service. Training in technical subjects should be concurrent with training in basic subjects. Training in elementary tactical subjects should not be postponed pending attainment of a high standard of proficiency in basic disciplinary training and the care and use of weapons. Concurrent training in different subjects affords variety and stimulates the interest of the soldier.

14. TACTICAL EXERCISES OF UNITS.—In the early stages of training, each tactical exercise is limited to a definite phase of combat. Attempts to cover several phases in a short period are rarely remunerative. Critique of tactical exercises is based upon the manuals or regulations. Tactical exercises of units should include combat situations where the units are operating with supported flanks as well as acting alone on detached missions. The tendency to devote excessive attention to situations of the unit acting alone or semi-independently to the neglect of instruction of the unit operating as a part of a larger force must be controlled. Rehearsed tactical exercises are prohibited.

From FM 21-20, *Physical Training* (1941)

4. PHYSICAL TRAINING PROGRAM.—*a. Scope.*—The physical training program described in this manual is composed of several different activities, each having a special purpose. The activities may be conducted either without the aid of equipment or with the aid of such as may be improvised. These activities are—

(1) Disciplinary exercises.

(2) Setting-up exercises.

(3) Marching and exercises while marching.

(4) Running, jumping, and climbing.

(5) Personal contests.

(6) Mass athletics and group games.

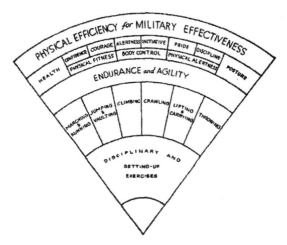

Physical efficiency matrix.

(7) Rifle exercises.

(8) Swimming.

b. Description and purpose.—(1) *Disciplinary exercises.*—These embrace the positions of attention, rests, facings, hand salute, mark time and halt, and the starting positions for setting-up exercises. These exercises must be executed with snap and precision. They are given at the very beginning of the daily morning period in physical training and are designed to give the instructor complete control over his unit as well as to alert the men for the work to follow.

(2) *Setting-up exercises.*—These exercises are for all parts of the body, arms, neck, shoulders, trunk, and legs. All are employed in each lesson in the harmonious development of the entire body. They serve not only to develop all parts of the body, but also as a warm-up to prepare the soldier for the more strenuous exercises which follow immediately after. Properly executed, they also have an educational and disciplinary value which is equal, if not superior, to the purely physiological benefits.

(3) *Marching and exercises while marching.*—These exercises consist of marching in quick or double time, and such exercises as can be performed while marching. They are designed to develop poise, posture, coordination, control, suppleness, and endurance.

(4) *Running, jumping, climbing, and crawling.*—This phase of the physical training program consists of work on the obstacle course, or, if no obstacle course is available, in traversing rough and varied terrain. It is designed to develop endurance,

agility, and coordination, as well as to train the soldier to overcome such obstacles as may confront him during field service.

(5) *Personal contests.*—Personal contests are the simpler forms of competitive gymnastics, where the participants are pitted against each other. Such contests never fail to produce rivalry for superiority. Their chief value lies in the development of agility and quickness of thought and action.

(6) *Mass athletics and group games.*—Mass athletics and group games are those forms of competitive or recreational sports which can be indulged in by all the men of a unit. They develop mental and physical alertness, coordination, and unit or group spirit, and give variety and interest to the physical training program.

(7) *Rifle exercises.*—Rifle exercises are in reality setting-up exercises with the rifle as equipment. Owing to the weight of the rifle, these exercises are useful for the development of the muscles of the arms, upper back, shoulders, and chest, and, when taken in conjunction with trunk and leg exercises they are excellent agents for the all-around development of those who possess the strength to wield the piece to advantage.

(8) *Swimming.*—Swimming is of importance to everyone connected with the service, and all officers and enlisted men should become proficient in it. Aside from its usefulness, it is an excellent means to all-around physical development.

(9) *Activities requiring special equipment.*—Activities requiring special equipment are not included in this manual. Activities of this type are—

(*a*) *Gymnastics.*—This includes exercises utilizing the horse, parallel bars, horizontal bar, rope, etc. The chief object of this instruction should be the development of the ability of the soldier to control his body while his weight is supported by or suspended from the arms and hands, thus enabling him to overcome such obstacles as may present themselves during field service. These exercises will tend to make the soldier agile and active and will teach him decision and self-reliance.

(*b*) *Boxing and wrestling.*—Boxing and wrestling develop endurance, agility, and strength, and are important factors in the development of confidence, courage, and self-control.

5. STANDARDS AND TESTS.—*a. Standards.*—[…] the physical training program should be based upon the condition and aptitude of the men to be trained. The best method of determining this condition and aptitude of the group is by comparison with known standards.

(1) The following table of standards may be used as a guide for men in field uniform:

Event	Minimum standard	Average	Above average	Superior
100-yard dash	14 seconds	13 seconds	$12^3/_5$ seconds	$12^1/_5$ seconds
Running high jump	3 feet 9 inches	4 feet	4 feet 4 inches	4 feet 6 inches
Running broad jump	12 feet	13 feet 6 inches	15 feet	16 feet 6 inches
Push-up from ground	20	25	30	35

(2) Other minimum standards for average men are—

(*a*) Baseball throw—125 feet.

(*b*) Basketball throw—60 feet.

(*c*) Bar or fence vault—4 feet.

(*d*) Run a quarter mile—87 seconds.

(*e*) Run a half mile—3 minutes 15 seconds.

(*f*) Walk 2 miles—23 minutes 30 seconds.

(*g*) Jump and reach—13 inches.

> 1. From a position with the feet close together and heels and toes on the ground, the man stretches both arms overhead, fingers extended. Measure this height.
>
> 2. He then jumps vertically, reaching as high as possible. Measure this height.
>
> 3. The difference between the heights in 1 and 2 above gives the "jump and reach" distance.

(*h*) Pull-up (chin)—6 times.

(*i*) Climb 20-foot rope—20 seconds.

(*j*) Standing hop, step and jump—18 feet.

(*k*) Running hop, step and jump—22 feet.

(*l*) Standing broad jump—6 feet.

(*m*) Standing backward jump—2 feet 8 inches.

(*n*) Running long dive—5 feet 6 inches.

b. Tests.—(1) The only way a comparison can be made between a standard to be reached and the ability of an individual or group is by tests. Tests have a very important place in any physical training program. They give the soldier an opportunity to compare his ability with that of others and, consequently, are of tremendous value in stimulating his interest and his effort. Tests serve the instructor as a means of measuring the progress of his men and the efficiency of his instruction. They also serve to point out to the instructor specific needs or deficiencies of individual men which require special instruction or corrective work.

(2) Tests can be conducted with little, if any, interference with the scheduled program, and require nothing more than a little planning on the part of the instructor. Their value to the program is so great that they should be held at regular intervals.

6. ALLOTMENT OF TIME FOR PHYSICAL TRAINING.—The time allotted to physical training for recruits should, when the training schedule permits, consists of 1½ hours each day. On the other hand, technical and tactical training requirements as approved in Mobilization Training Programs must be met, and the desired 1½ hours of physical training daily may have to be reduced. It is the task of the commander concerned to utilize to maximum advantage, the time available for physical training. A brief description of how a daily 1½-hour physical training period may be successfully employed is given in *a* and *b* below.

a. Morning period.—(1) The morning period should begin not earlier than 1 hour after breakfast and should last at least 30 minutes. Men should not be required to indulge in strenuous exercises before breakfast. Exercises before breakfast are not recommended; if indulged in at all, they should be confined to a few arm stretchings and relaxed trunk-bending exercises—just exertion enough to accelerate circulation mildly. To exercise strenuously before breakfast is likely to affect the digestive operation seriously, and is more apt to weaken than to strengthen the body, which is at a very low state of physical efficiency immediately after arising, when its resistance is low. It has been shown that the body does not regain its normal state of physical efficiency until well after breakfast and that it reaches its highest peak of efficiency in the middle of the afternoon.

(2) The morning period should embrace the following forms of exercise in the order named:

(*a*) Disciplinary exercises, 2 or 3 minutes.

(*b*) Setting-up exercises, 12 to 15 minutes.

(*c*) Marching and exercises while marching, 3 to 5 minutes.

(*d*) Running, jumping, climbing, etc. (work on the obstacle course), 8 to 10 minutes.

(*e*) If more than 30 minutes are available, add personal contests.

(*f*) At times it is desirable to substitute personal contests and group games for (*c*) and (*d*) above, even though only 30 minutes are available for the period.

b. Afternoon period.—The afternoon period should be closely supervised but should be primarily recreational. It should be devoted to conducting tests, mass athletics, and group games. Where facilities exist for swimming, gymnastics, boxing, and wrestling, such instruction should be given at this time.

7. UNIFORM TO BE WORN.—*a.* The uniform worn will depend upon the season of the year and the state of the weather. At no time should a uniform be worn which does not admit of the freest possible movement of the body.

b. Undershirts, slacks, or loosely laced breeches without leggings, and regulation shoes comprise the usual uniform during the summer months; olive-drab shirts are usually prescribed during cold or inclement weather. Hats, caps, or blouses should not be worn.

8. ELEMENTARY RULES FOR HEALTH.—*a.* Health is that quality of the entire body, including the mind, which renders the soldier capable of developing to the highest degree of efficiency. Good health, denoting a vigorous body, alert mind, and high morale, is evidenced by the degree in which it expresses itself in a well-disciplined, proud, confident, and capable soldier. Physical health cannot be separated from mental health. Ill health is quite as often due to conditions of the mind resulting in bodily ailment as due to purely physical causes. Therefore, in giving rules for health, it is essential that mental hygiene as well as physical hygiene be considered.

b. A healthy state of mind is characterized by cheerfulness, confidence, and interest. An unhealthy state of mind is characterized by indifference, discouragement, worry, and a feeling of inferiority due to lack of success or progress. Much can be done through physical training to develop in the men a healthy mental state. This may be accomplished by—

(1) Instructor being a worthy example to the men.

(2) A fair, impartial, understanding attitude on the part of the instructor.

(3) Work being interesting and varied.

(4) Work being arranged so as to result in progressive development.

c. The importance of proper personal habits, such as cleanliness, proper eating, rest, and elimination, should be stressed to the men during instruction in physical training.

d. Physical training should not be scheduled immediately after reveille or immediately before or after meals.

e. Clothing suitable for exercise should be prescribed.

f. Men should be "warmed up" gradually before engaging in strenuous exercise.

g. Muscular action produces an unusual amount of bodily heat which should be lost gradually, otherwise the body will be chilled. Hence, after exercise, never remove clothing to cool off, but, on the contrary, wear some additional clothing. If no additional clothing is available, men should be kept mildly active allowing the body to cool gradually.

h. Drinking water, particularly cold water, during or immediately after exercise should be discouraged; the body should be allowed to recover its normal condition before quenching the thirst with draughts of cold water. If necessary to do so while exercising, cool, not cold, water may be used in small quantities, but exercise must continue, especially if the body is in a state of perspiration.

U.S. Army obstacle course.

Training Notes for the Recent Fighting in Tunisia is an interesting document from late 1943, in which the Army attempted to translate frontline combat experience and firsthand testimony into practical advice for training units. The Army's bruising first few months in North Africa had illustrated the gulf between theory and reality, and also the fact that while soldiers could be trained to go through the motions for combat, they had to train with urgency and realism if their instruction was to keep them alive on the frontlines. The document below, therefore, carries a genuine sense of urgency and relevance.

One problem inherent in the U.S. Army training system during World War II was the efficacy of the Replacement Training Centers (RTC), in which individuals were trained purely to act as replacements for frontline units stripped out by combat losses. The recruits at the RTCs were trained in military procedures plus the basic specialisms of the branch to which they assigned (all the men within an RTC company would be instructed in the same specialism to improve the efficiency of training). Yet the urgency to fill out depleted combat units often meant that the RTC recruits had their training programs cut short, and they were posted, woefully unprepared, to the frontline, having to slot in alongside hardened veterans who often had little emotional energy to spend bringing a green recruit up to speed on how to survive. Casualties amongst the replacements were therefore predictably dreadful.

From *Training Notes for the Recent Fighting in Tunisia* (1943)

I. INFANTRY AND OTHER ARMS

1. DIGGING IN

Almost all officers and unit commanders interviewed agreed that their units lacked initial training in the necessity and technique of digging in under actual combat conditions. Many agreed that this is a lesson quickly learned, but the first lesson often proves costly in casualties. There was general agreement that this lack of training was largely a result of failure to dig in realistically during maneuvers. Too often maneuver training permitted only outlining of foxholes, slit trenches, gun pits, etc. General opinion is that unit must be trained to dig in, and that they must have this training before entering the combat zone. Officers and men interviewed commented as follows:

[…]

"… The men did not dig in. They were ordered to at once upon reaching the position. but they delayed, talked, and gathered in groups. They seemed to have the idea—'it'll be time enough when the shooting starts.' Then when the shells came over, they all started to dig in at once, and there were not enough shovels to go round …"

—Chaplain Kines
3rd Bn., 39th Infantry

"… We didn't know what it meant to dig until we came out here. The men were just not convinced of the necessity of digging until they were shelled or bombed. We used to tape outlines of trenches and positions in the maneuvers. The lesson is often costly …"

—Lt. Colonel Sylvester, 151st F.A. Bn., with Executive Officer and S-3

[…]

2. CAMOUFLAGE, CONCEALMENT AND COVER

[…]

"… Camouflage—use all natural material in addition to nets, and above all, use proper dispersion. We never understood what dispersion was until we got over here. During the battle of FAID, a small battalion action, we dispersed our vehicles in normal 'maneuver' dispersion distance in the only grove of trees there was around there. Then around seven o'clock in the morning, known as 'Stuka time', one Ju 88 flew over and circled us one, and on successive flights, about five in all, we lost nine vehicles—four 2½-ton trucks and five Jeeps. This happened in less than ten minutes' time. After this we learned what dispersion really was. Fortunately we

U.S. soldiers land ashore in Algiers during Operation *Torch*, 1942.

have learned the use of slit trenches, and lost no men in this incident. Only one man, attempting to put out the fire in his Jeep, was hit in the leg by a machine gun bullet from a plane ... Where there is no cover, use the natural folds in the terrain and disperse ..."

—Lt. Colonel Bowen
Ex.O., 26th Infantry

[...]

3. SCOUTING, PATROLLING AND NIGHT OPERATIONS

In almost all units visited, the necessity of more training in scouting, patrolling, and operations at night was stressed. The infantry commanders and officers agreed that our units have been especially weak in these phases of training, and strongly recommend that they be emphasized in the training of all units prior to their entering the combat zone. In the artillery units the need of more training in night reconnaissance and night operations of all kinds was brought out. A majority of officers interviewed concurred that the German and Italian troops have no liking for night fighting and a strengthening of our troops in this work will give us material advantage. Officers and men interviewed commented as follows:

"... More emphasis should be given to night operations, especially patrolling ... There should be more intensive and practical training in the conduct of the individual soldier in day and night patrolling. Compared to the French we are amateurs in patrolling. Men need more training in practical terrain appreciation in patrol work. Teach men to hold their fire until they definitely have targets ..."

—Lt. Colonel Cunningham, 1st Bn.,
16th Infantry, Staff, and Company Commanders

"… The most important element of training for the infantry in this campaign is patrolling, all phases of it night and day. I cannot emphasise this too much … In our battalion we have organised a 'combat patrol squad' per company, composed of the best all around men, men good with the rifle, with grenades, and specially in scouting. We use these squads for important and difficult missions. They are composed of picked volunteers, always the best men. These squads have always proved reliable, night and day, and have proved excellent in results. The ideal would be to develop eventually all squads in the companies along the same lines. They also provide a fine proving ground for non-coms …

"… For night attacks, train your men in proper methods—slow, silent, creeping movement to within bayonet range of the enemy. Teach men the proper use of the crew weapons, to place the enemy in a sort of box barrage of fire so he cannot get out … and then close on him with the bayonet …

"… We needed also more training in real light discipline in night operations. The promiscuous use of flashlights and matches—things that got by in maneuvers—won't do up here where any light will give away a position … stress this in training and make men adhere to real light discipline such as we have had to learn up here …"

—Lt. Colonel Cunningham,
1st Bn., 16th Infantry

"… In training, emphasize night operations, particularly night patrol work. Train intensively on the old 'sneakin' and 'peepin' and how to distinguish and identify different sounds. Teach men to move cautiously and silently—to crawl noiselessly. Train them in accurate use of the compass night and day, and in map reading—not just learning facts about maps by rote, but in the practical field use of maps. Also train them in the technique of observation. Half the information we get is from observation and patrolling …

"… In contact during night operations and patrolling the best weapons are the Thompson sub-machine gun and the Browning automatic rifle. Our men swear by them for night work …

"… one important battle lesson has been the failure of junior officers to be ice-clear and specific in instructions and directions, especially with regard to patrolling, scouting, and night operations …

"… For night operations, a prior daylight reconnaissance must be made. We have found officers and men lacking in adequate training in reconnaissance. Without adequate daylight reconnaissance, night patrols often get lost. In one instance failure to reconnoiter a position and an area for a night operation resulted in a patrol being ambushed by outposts unknown to the patrol leader and his men …

"… In all night operations, have a single objective. Never split a night patrol—always keep it intact. Use more than one patrol if the mission requires two groups, but keep those patrols intact themselves …

"… In training before arriving in the combat zone, incorporate realism into the night patrolling and scouting. Teach men patience. Make them sit motionless, lie motionless, for several hours on outpost and in observation posts, they'll have to learn patience and this sort of thing in actual combat, so start it in their basic training …

"… Make men learn to take off their helmets when on night patrol. Our present type of helmet greatly magnifies sounds and causes men under tension to imagine they hear all sorts of sounds. Also the helmet in brushing against twigs or underbrush will make noises that may give the position away …

"… Let every man on scout and patrol know the situation clearly. He must know it in order to carry out his part. Also give each man a definite mission, a definite job and the responsibility for carrying it out …

"… An all-important point in all scouting, observation, and reconnaissance patrolling. Train men to report only <u>what they actually see</u>, and not to include any personal interpretations. Make the essential details complete, but let the topside people do the interpreting. If they report information they didn't see personally, report the data absolutely as given, and who gave it. One outstanding example-lesson was the twisting of information reported. An OP reported that they had seen three <u>Italians</u> coming down a certain hill. This information was given to someone else for relaying to a higher headquarters. It was reported that three <u>battalions</u> were coming down the hill. Clarity of reports and certainty of the proper understanding of reports must be stressed …"

—S-2, 16th Infantry

[…]

4. FIELD HARDENING OF TROOPS

The need for real field hardening of the individual soldier before entering the combat zone was stressed in most of the units visited. Several officers and unit commanders urged that more practical and realistic training be given to troops to prepare them for the tests of physical endurance, stamina and hardships of combat operations. Officers and men interviewed commented as follows:

"… Make your men march in full pack, without water, under realistic, hard conditions. Take men out for training operations in the blackest nights, in the worst weather, under the worst conditions, over the most difficult terrain. Make this progressive, of course, but in their training lead up to these conditions. Emphasize cross country marches, get off the roads, the easy routes. Roads are often mined, impassable, strafed by planes, and not usable ...

"... We learned the hard way in the Scottish mountains, and we are now hard, really hard. In the operations against GAFSA [a German-held town in Tunisia] we had to reach an objective over high, rocky mountains—several ridges of them. We could take no transportation, and we had to streamline our heavy weapons company. We took only two .50-caliber squads in lieu of anti-tank weapons, and these we carried by hand. All ammunition had to be carried by hand. No resupply was possible, and we could make no provision for medical evacuation. We used cooks, supply sergeants, company clerks, and anyone who could walk to carry weapons and ammunition. We laid 14 miles of wire by hand, all of which was carried by hand. It gave out five miles short of our objective, and we bridged the gap by radio. The total march was 17 miles over some seven or eight mountain ridges. After this we went into position for attack. It is of interest that the map distance was 8 miles. The terrain extended our march to 17 miles. We measured out 14 miles of it with our wire. We left our assembly area at 4:00 a.m. and reached our line of departure and formed for the attack by 2:00 p.m. The only casualty was one man with a sprained ankle but he got there late. It takes hard men to do such a march as this. Train your men to be able to do the same and their training will fit them for real combat ..."

—Lt. Colonel Cunningham, 1st Bn.,
16th Infantry, Staff, and Company Commanders

[...]

5. TRAINING IN MINE WARFARE

The general consensus of opinion in the units visited reveals that there is definite need for training in all arms in mind detecting, clearing and removal. This was true of engineers, infantry, and artillery. In the artillery and infantry units it was pointed out that often operations must be carried out in places and at times when the services of engineer detachments are not available. Unit commanders and officers stressed the need of practical training in the United States, before units arrive in the theater of operations. the infantry and artillery officers feel that mine detectors should be included in their TBA [Table of Basic Allowance]. Officers and men interviewed commented as follows:

[...]

"… Men need more training in handling explosives, mines, and booby traps, detecting and clearing them. We need more mine detectors and men trained in their use …"

—Colonel Fechet, 16th Infantry

"… Mines and booby traps: The training in the defensive use of mines and in the passing of minefields was inadequate prior to our entering combat … in a flank movement on GAFSA the one Engineer platoon attached to a battalion combat team cleared 400 mines from six different fields. They were so thick that I couldn't tell where one field began and another ended. We lost four vehicles and I had to take my column off the road entirely and go across country. When going through mined areas, get off the roads and make your own road. We use sandbags in vehicles. They are not entirely effective, but they reduce casualties, although the vehicles may be wrecked. Engineer sandbags half-filled and laid flat on the floors and worked up all around, especially the transmission and well up under the dashboard … I strongly recommend far more realistic, practical training in mine and booby trap detection and removal …"

—Lt. Colonel Bowen
26th Infantry

U.S. soldiers of the 16th Infantry, Kasserine Pass, 1943.

For the new U.S. Army infantryman, overseas deployment fostered both anxiety and excitement, the former because of the prospect of seeing combat, the latter because it offered for many an unprecedented opportunity to see the wider world. The U.S. military authorities, concerned that millions of U.S. personnel act appropriately as ambassadors for the armed services and the United States as a whole, issued various pamphlets and booklets that attempted to educate the soldiers about the various dos and don'ts when in a foreign culture. The first extract is from *Instructions for American Servicemen in Britain* (1942). The UK was, between 1943 and 1944, transformed into a huge overseas base for the United States, with some 1.5 million GIs spending time there, typically before deployment on to mainland Europe following the D-Day landings in June 1944. The advice given is sensitive and balanced, not least the injunction that the U.S. soldiers appreciate the fact that Britain had already been at war for three or four years by the time the U.S. soldiers arrived. The second extract, from *Short Guide to Iraq* (1943), had a very different context, as it was written for the relatively small numbers of U.S. troops posted to Iraq on security duties during the war. Its advice has a rather timeless quality, so much so that many U.S. soldiers deployed to Iraq following the 2003 invasion found that it still offered sage guidance on the meeting between American and Islamic culture.

From *Instructions for American Servicemen in Britain* (1942)

BRITISH RESERVED, NOT UNFRIENDLY. You defeat enemy propaganda not by denying that these differences exist, but by admitting them openly and then trying to understand them. For instance: The British are often more reserved in conduct than we. On a small, crowded island where forty-five million people live, each man learns to guard his privacy carefully—and is equally careful not to invade another man's privacy.

So if Britons sit in trains or busses without striking up conversation with you, it doesn't mean they are being haughty and unfriendly. Probably they are paying more attention to you than you think. But they don't speak to you because they don't want to appear intrusive or rude.

Another difference. The British have phrases and colloquialisms of their own that may sound funny to you. You can make just as many boners [stupid mistakes] in their eyes. It isn't a good idea, for instance, to say "bloody" in mixed company in Britain—it is one of their worst swear words. To say: "I look like a bum" is offensive to their ears, for to the British this means that you look like your own backside; it isn't important—just a tip if you are trying to shine in polite society. […]

British money is in pounds, shillings, and pence. […] The British are used to this system and they like it, and all your arguments that the American decimal system is better won't convince them. They won't be pleased to hear you call it "funny money," either. They sweat hard to get it (wages are much lower in Britain than America) and they won't think you smart or funny for mocking at it.

DON'T BE A SHOW OFF. The British dislike bragging and showing off. American wages and American soldier's pay are the highest in the world. When pay day comes it would be sound practice to learn to spend your money according to British standards. They consider you highly paid. They won't think any better of you for throwing money around; they are more likely to feel that you haven't learned the common-sense virtues of thrift. The British "Tommy" is apt to be specially touchy about the difference between his wages and yours. Keep this in mind. Use common sense and don't rub him the wrong way.

You will find many things in Britain physically different from similar things in America. But there are also important similarities—our common speech, our common law, and our ideals of religious freedom were all brought from Britain when the Pilgrims landed at Plymouth Rock. Our ideas about political liberties are also British and parts of our own Bill of Rights were borrowed from the great charters of British liberty.

Remember that in America you like people to conduct themselves as we do, and to respect the same things. Try to do the same for the British and respect the things they treasure.

THE BRITISH ARE TOUGH. Don't be misled by the British tendency to be soft-spoken and polite. If they need to be, they can be plenty tough. The English language didn't spread across the oceans and over the mountains and jungles and swamps of the world because these people were panty-waists.

Sixty thousand British civilians—men, women, and children—have died under bombs, and yet the morale of the British is unbreakable and high. A nation doesn't come through that, if it doesn't have plain, common guts. The British are tough, strong people, and good allies.

You won't be able to tell the British much about "taking it." They are not particularly interested in taking it any more. They are far more interested in getting together in solid friendship with us, so that we can all start dishing it out to Hitler.

[…]

REMEMBER THERE'S A WAR ON. Britain may look a little shop-worn and grimy to you. The British people are anxious to have you know that you are not seeing their country at its best. There's been a war on since 1939. The houses haven't been painted because factories are not making paint—they're making planes. The famous English gardens and parks are either unkept because there are no men to take care of them, or they are being used to grow needed vegetables. British taxicabs look antique because Britain makes tanks for herself and Russia and hasn't time to make new cars. British trains are cold because power is needed for industry, not for heating. There are no luxury dining cars on trains because total war effort has no place for such frills. The trains are unwashed and grimy because men and women are needed for more important work than car-washing. The British people are anxious for you to know that in normal times Britain looks much prettier, cleaner, neater.

[…]

THE PEOPLE—THEIR CUSTOMS AND MANNERS

THE BEST WAY to get on in Britain is very much the same as the best way to get on in America. The same sort of courtesy and decency and friendliness that go over big in America will go over big in Britain. The British have seen a good many Americans and they like Americans. They will like your frankness as long as it is friendly. They will expect you to be generous. They are not given to back-slapping and they are shy about showing their affections. But once they get to like you they make the best friends in the world. In "getting along" the first important thing to remember is that the British are like the Americans in many ways—but not in all ways. You are quickly discovering differences that seem confusing and even wrong. Like driving on the left side of the road, and having money based on an "impossible" accounting system, and drinking warm beer. But once you get used to things like that, you will realize that they belong to England just as baseball and jazz and coco-cola belong to us.

[…]

KEEP OUT OF ARGUMENTS. You can rub a Britisher the wrong way by telling him "we came over and won the last one." Each nation did its share. But Britain remembers that nearly a million of her best manhood died in the last war. America lost 60,000 in action.

Such arguments and the war debts along with them are dead issues. Nazi propaganda now is pounding away day and night asking the British people why they should fight "to save Uncle Shylock and his silver dollar." Don't play into Hitler's hands by mentioning war debts.

Neither do the British need to be told that their armies lost the first couple of rounds in the present war. We've lost a couple, ourselves, so do not start off by being critical of them and saying what the Yanks are going to do. Use your head before you sound off, and remember how long the British alone held Hitler off without any help from anyone.

In the pubs you will hear a lot of Britons openly criticizing their Government and the conduct of the war. That isn't an occasion for you to put in your two-cents worth. It's their business, not yours. You sometimes criticize members of your own family— but just let an outsider start doing the same, and you know how you feel!

The Briton is just as outspoken and independent as we are. But don't get him wrong. He is also the most law abiding citizen in the world, because the British system of justice is just about the best there is. There are fewer murders, robberies, and burglaries in the whole of Great Britain in a year than in a single large American city.

Once again, look, listen, and learn before you start telling the British how much better we do things. They will be interested to hear about life in America and you have a great chance to overcome the picture many of them have gotten from the movies of an America made up of wild Indians and gangsters. When you find differences between British and American ways of doing things, there is usually a good reason for them.

[…]

SOME IMPORTANT DO'S AND DON'TS

BE FRIENDLY but don't intrude anywhere it seems you are not wanted. You will find the British money system easier than you think. A little study beforehand will make it still easier.

You are higher paid than the British "Tommy." Don't rub it in. Play fair with him. He can be a pal in need.

Don't show off or brag or bluster—"swank" as the British say. If somebody looks in your direction and says, "he's chucking his weight about," you can be pretty sure you're off base. That's the time to pull in your ears.

If you are invited to eat with a family don't eat too much. Otherwise you may eat up their weekly rations.

Don't make fun of British speech or accents. You sound just as funny to them but they are too polite to show it.

Avoid comments on the British Government or politics.

Don't try to tell the British that America won the last war or make wise-cracks about the war debts or about British defeats in this war.

NEVER criticize the King or Queen.

Don't criticize the food, beer, or cigarettes to the British. Remember they have been at war since 1939.

Use common sense on all occasions. By your conduct you have great power to bring about a better understanding between the two countries after the war is over.

You will soon find yourself among a kindly, quiet, hardworking people who have been living under a strain such as few people in the world have ever known. In your dealings with them, let this be your slogan:

It is always impolite to criticize your hosts; it is militarily stupid to criticize your allies.

From *Short Guide to Iraq* (1943)

MEET THE PEOPLE

[…] Most Americans and Europeans who have gone to Iraq didn't like it at first. Might as well be frank about it. They thought it a harsh, hot, parched, dusty, and inhospitable land. But nearly all of these same people changed their minds after a few days or weeks, and largely on account of the Iraqi people they began to meet. So will you.

That tall man in the flowing robe you are going to see soon, with the whiskers and the long hair, is a first-class fighting man, highly skilled in guerrilla warfare. Few fighters in any country, in fact, excel him in that kind of situation. If he is your friend, he can be a staunch and valuable ally. If he should happen to be your enemy—look out! Remember Lawrence of Arabia? Well, it was with men like these that he wrote history in the First World War.

But you will also find out quickly that the Iraqi is one of the most cheerful and friendly people in the world. Few people you have seen get so much fun out of work and everyday living. If you are willing to go just a little out of your way to understand him, everything will be o. k.

Differences? Of Course! Differences? Sure, there are differences. Differences of costume. Differences of food. Differences of manner and custom and religious beliefs. Different attitudes toward women. Differences galore.

But what of it? You aren't going to Iraq to change the Iraqis. Just the opposite. We are fighting this war to preserve the principle of "live and let live." Maybe that sounded like a lot of words to you at home. Now you have a chance to prove it to yourself and others. If you can, it's going to be a better world to live in for all of us.

Although relatively few Iraqis receive a formal education similar to yours, they are shrewd and intelligent and tend to believe what they hear and see with their own ears and eyes. By what you do and how you act you can do a lot to win this war and the peace after it. Right now Iraq is threatened with invasion—as America is now. The Iraqis have some religious and tribal differences among themselves. Hitler has been trying to use these differences to his own ends. If you can win the trust and friendship of all the Iraqis you meet, you will do more than you may think possible to help bring them together in our common cause.

Needless to say, Hitler will also try to use the differences between ourselves and Iraqis to make trouble. But we have a weapon to beat that kind of thing. Plain common horse sense. Let's use it.

Hitler's game is to divide and conquer. Ours is to unite and win!

[…]

CLIMATE AND HEALTH—SANITARY CONDITIONS

IRAQ is a hot country. This means: keep your headgear on when you are in the summer sun. In this kind of a climate it is very easy to let yourself be burned and think nothing of it. But next day you are likely to wake up with black blisters and possible fever. The headgear issued to you will be sufficient to protect you. But whatever you wear, be sure that it shades the back of your neck as well as the top of your head. If you expose the back of your neck you are inviting sunstroke. Don't, under any circumstances, take a sun bath.

In the desert, be prepared for extremes of temperature. The days are usually very hot. The nights can be uncomfortably cool.

Boil your drinking water or see that it is properly chlorinated. You will find that conditions of life in Iraq do not allow the degree of sanitation or cleanliness that we know.

Avoid eating unwashed vegetables and fruits. They may be contaminated by human excrement. Wash raw fruits and vegetables in water or alcohol or peel them before eating them, because the skins may have become contaminated by flies or by human contact. Avoid leafy vegetables altogether. Keep all food away from flies.

Diseases: Malaria and typhoid are two very serious fevers. You should guard against them in every possible way. Malaria is carried by a particular kind of mosquito which breeds in marshy areas, uncovered wells and cisterns and in shallow water pools. If at all possible, stay away from areas in which malaria is common. When you can't do this, sleep under nets and keep your arms and legs covered, especially at dusk.

Typhoid is contracted from unboiled water and from raw foods which have not been properly cleaned or peeled. Once again, avoid them.

Sandflies, which are smaller than mosquitos and which can get through an ordinary mosquito net, carry a slight three-day fever which is not serious but is very weakening. It is known as sandfly fever. Sandflies are most prevalent in midsummer. Coating yourself with a light oil will give you some protection from them.

You should be very careful about bugs and lice, which are common. Give yourself a frequent once-over for them. Scabies is a skin infection, produced by a parasite which feeds on the skin. It is extremely annoying and difficult to get rid of. However, it can be cured by sulphur ointment.

Intestinal diseases, such as dysentery and tapeworm, are very common in Iraq. These can be avoided, or at least made less severe, by extreme care in the water you drink and the food you eat.

Trachoma, a very common disease of the eye, can be picked up almost everywhere, even from shaking hands with someone and then touching your eyes. *Don't rub or touch your eyes.*

Toilets such as those in America are very scarce. You will have to get used to relieving yourself outdoors at any convenient spot. Be sure to get well off the main streets and well away from mosques, and out of sight as much as possible. You will have to carry your own supply of toilet paper.

There is a good deal of venereal disease around, so don't take chances.

[…]

SOME IMPORTANT DO'S AND DON'TS

Keep away from mosques.

Smoke or spit somewhere else—never in front of a mosque.

If you come near a mosque, keep moving (away) and don't loiter.

Keep silent when the Moslems are praying (which they do five times a day) and don't stare.

Discuss something else—NEVER religion or politics or women—with Moslems.

Remember the fear of the "evil eye." Don't stare at anyone. Don't point your camera in anyone's face.

Avoid offering opinions on internal politics.

Shake hands with the Iraqi; otherwise don't touch them or slap them on the back.

Remember that the Iraqi are a very modest people and avoid any exposure of the body in their presence.

Keep out of the sun whenever you can. When you can't, keep your head and neck covered.

Start eating only after your host has begun.

Eat with your right hand—never with your left, even if you are a southpaw.

Always tear bread with your fingers—never cut it.

Bread to the Moslems is holy. Don't throw scraps of it about or let it fall on the ground.

In the city eat only part of the first course. There may be more coming.

In the country leave some food in the bowl—what you leave goes to the women and children.

Don't offer Moslems food containing pork, bacon, or lard, or cooked in pork products. All such food is religiously "unclean" to them.

Don't eat pork or pork products in front of Moslems.

Be pleasant if Moslems refuse to eat meat you offer.

Don't offer Moslems alcoholic drinks. Drink liquor somewhere else—never in the presence of Moslems.

Knock before entering a private house. If a woman answers, wait until she has had time to retire.

Always respect the Moslem women. Don't stare at them. Don't smile at them. Don't talk to them or follow them. If you do any of these things, it means trouble for you and your unit.

In a house or tent, follow the rule of your host. If he takes off his shoes on entering, do the same.

If you are required to sit on the floor in an Iraqi house or tent, cross your legs while doing so.

When visiting, don't overstay your welcome. The third glass of tea or coffee is the signal to leave unless you are quartered there.

If you should see grown men walking hand in hand, ignore it. They are not "queer."

Be kind and considerate to servants. The Iraqis consider all people equals.

Avoid any expression of race prejudice. The people draw very little color line.

Talk Arabic if you can to the people. No matter how badly you do it, they will like it.

Shake hands on meeting and leaving.

On meeting an Iraqi, be sure to inquire after his health.

If you wish to give someone a present, make it sweets or cigarettes.

If you are stationed in the country, it is a good idea to take sweets and cigarettes with you when you visit an Iraqi's home.

Be polite. Good manners are important to the Iraqis. Be hospitable.

Bargain on prices. Don't let shopkeepers or merchants overcharge you; but be polite.

Be generous with your cigarettes.

Above all, use common sense on all occasions. And remember that every American soldier is an unofficial ambassador of good will.

CHAPTER 3

INFANTRY WEAPONS AND EQUIPMENT

One strength the U.S. Army always brought to the fight in World War II was firepower. Partly this was due to the massive outputs of U.S. armament factories, which included 102,410 tanks and self-propelled guns, 257,390 artillery pieces, 105,055 mortars, nearly 2.7 million machine guns, and 5.4 million M1 Garand rifles. But the mass of U.S. firepower was also explained by sensible war production choices, the U.S. war machine opting to produce fewer types of solid-performing weapon systems on a huge scale rather than go down the German route of the over-proliferation of types.

A U.S. infantry rifle company included three rifle platoons, whose principal weapons were the M1 Garand rifle, M1 Carbine and Browning Automatic Rifle (BAR), the latter for light assault support fire, albeit limited by its 20-round box magazine. A weapons platoon boosted the support fire through a vehicle-mounted .50-cal Browning M2HB machine gun, two .30-cal Browning M1919A4 light machine guns, and one 60mm mortar. The wider infantry battalion also had a full weapons company, which included two heavy machine-gun (HMG) platoons and one 81mm mortar platoon. The battalion's antitank platoon was equipped with either the 37mm M3 or 57mm M1 antitank guns.

When all this firepower was brought together in a coordinated fashion, the effect on target could be devastating. FM 7-5 below outlines the basic capabilities of the infantry weapon systems, both individual and crew-served. It also goes on to describe some of the other equipment utilized within the rifle battalion. In this work, written in 1940, it is notable that the prospect of gas attack was still present in military thinking, thankfully one outcome that didn't materialize in an otherwise ghastly war.

From FM 7-5, *Organization and Tactics of Infantry: The Rifle Battalion* (1940)

CHAPTER 2

SECTION I
INDIVIDUAL WEAPONS

15. RIFLE AND BAYONET.—*a.* The rifle is the primary weapon of the individual fighter. It is a flat-trajectory shoulder weapon suited for frontal fire and for use against distributed targets. Supplemented by the bayonet, it is the arm for hand-to-hand fighting. The rifle fires ball ammunition against personnel and airplanes. Its armor-piercing ammunition is effective against lightly armored vehicles or airplanes at close range. Tracer ammunition is used by leaders and scouts to point out targets and determine ranges and as an aid to antiaircraft (AA) fire control.

b. The semiautomatic rifle, M1, is capable of approximately 20 to 30 aimed shots a minute. The M1903 rifle is reloaded by hand operation of the bolt and is capable of a rate of about 10 to 15 rounds a minute.

16. AUTOMATIC RIFLE.—The automatic rifle is a rifle that fires ammunition on the automatic principle with recoil supported by the body of the firer. The Browning automatic rifle is capable of rapid production of a large volume of concentrated fire and offers a small target when in action. An automatic rifleman has the marching mobility but not the capacity for short bursts of speed of the rifleman. The automatic rifle is not suited for sustained fire for long periods or for indirect or overhead fire. In the attack, the difficulty of keeping the automatic rifle supplied with ammunition and its inferiority in combat mobility to the rifle lead to its retention as a reserve of automatic fire for use in the critical emergencies of combat to support the attack of the rifle squads. In defense, automatic rifles are the principal weapons of the rifle platoons, and except where the platoon is assigned an unusually wide sector of fire, they cover the entire platoon fire sector. By reason of their superior mobility, automatic rifles are used in preference to machine guns in advance of the outpost line of resistance. The automatic rifle is a particularly effective weapon against hostile aircraft at very low altitudes.

17. PISTOL.—The automatic pistol or the revolver is an arm of emergency and individual defense at close quarters (ranges up to 50 yards) for personnel not armed with the rifle or the automatic rifle. It is not suited to the purposes of collective action.

18. HAND GRENADE.—The hand grenade is a curved-trajectory weapon complementary to the rifle and bayonet of the individual skirmisher. It is used against an enemy sheltered behind cover to cause casualties or force him into the open. The

grenade is hand thrown. Its radius of effect is from 15 to 30 yards, depending on the type of grenade. Small particles capable of inflicting serious wounds may travel as far as 100 yards from the point of detonation. Its short range (30 to 45 yards) prevents the use in open warfare of grenades having a wide radius of effect. The difficulty of supply and distribution, together with the weight of the projectile, limits the number which can be carried by the soldier and restricts its offensive use. The difficulty of supply largely disappears in the defense. Special types of grenades are used for lachrymatory or irritating gases.

SECTION II
RANGES AND ALTITUDES

19. RANGES.—For general infantry purpose ranges are classified as follows:

	Yards
Short	Point blank to 200.
Close	200–400.
Midranges	400–600.
Long	600–1,500.
Distant	Beyond 1,500.

20. ALTITUDES.—Altitudes of aerial targets are designated as follows:

	Feet
Very low	0 to 200.
Low	200 to 1,000.
Medium	1,000 to 3,000.
High	Beyond 3,000.

SECTION III
CREW-SERVED WEAPONS

21. TRANSPORTATION.—Crew-served weapons and their ammunition are transported on motor weapon and ammunition carriers or pack animals. These regulations relate to infantry units equipped with motor transportation. In combat the weapons, except antitank (AT) gun, usually require manhandling; the carriers keep ammunition as close to the weapons as practicable.

22. MACHINE GUNS.—*a. General.*—The machine gun is a weapon that fires small-arms ammunition automatically with recoil supported by a fixed mount. Machine guns are classified as light and heavy machine guns (cal. .30) and antitank machine guns (cal. .50).

A vehicle-mounted Browning .50-cal M2HB machine gun.

b. Light.—The light machine gun is air-cooled and relatively mobile. Its crew can maintain the march rate of a rifleman but cannot move at the high speed of the individual rifleman. It delivers a large volume of fire rapidly and accurately. The capacity of the gun on its ground mount for overhead, indirect fire, and antiaircraft fires is limited. Its characteristics fit it for use in the attack for the close support of the smaller infantry units by flanking action; in defense, to supplement the action of heavy machine guns. Within midrange its accuracy is sensibly that of the heavy machine gun.

c. Heavy.—The heavy machine gun is water-cooled. Filled with water, it weighs 40 pounds. The mount weighs 52 pounds. The limit of the useful range is about 3,500 yards. Effective direct, aimed fire is limited by observation. Effective indirect fire is limited by the maximum range of the gun and the conditions for securing fire data. The heavy machine gun lacks the mobility of the light gun, but its more stable mount gives it greater accuracy at long ranges. It is capable of overhead and indirect fire and has great capacity for sustained fires. The latter characteristics render it preeminently the automatic weapon for use in the defense and for the delivery of protective fires in the attack. Over level or uniformly sloping ground, the danger space is continuous for a distance of 750 yards from the muzzle of the gun.

23. MANHANDLED ANTITANK WEAPONS.—*a.* Antitank weapons of the lighter class have the following general characteristics:

Weight of individual load, not in excess of 55 lbs.

Number of loads, two to three.

Armor penetration, ½ to 1 inch at 500 yards.

Rate of fire, automatic or semiautomatic.

Caliber, .50 to .80.

b. Antitank weapons in the lighter class must be sufficiently mobile to keep pace with the leading troops, independent of animal or motor transport. They vary widely in ballistic characteristics and power.

24. MORTARS.—*a. 60-mm.*—The 60-mm mortar is a highly mobile and accurate curved-trajectory weapon, using an explosive projectile weighing approximately 3½ pounds, with a useful range of about 1,000 yards. The barrel and tripod together weigh 28 pounds, the base plate 23 pounds. Its rate of fire may reach 20 rounds per minute. The weight of its ammunition exacts economy in expenditure in offensive operations. The mortar is adapted to overhead fire, to fire from masked positions, and to fires against defiladed targets. It is habitually employed close to the front line and is quickly adaptable to changes in the tactical situation of small rifle units.

b. 81-mm.—There are three shell for use with this weapon: a light explosive shell; a heavy explosive shell; and a heavy smoke shell. The light explosive shell has a useful range of 2,000 yards. The range is, however, limited by observation rather than the ballistic properties of the piece. The heavy explosive shell used against materiel and emplacements has a maximum range of 1,500 yards. The barrel, bipod, and base plate each weigh approximately 45 pounds. Compared with the 60-mm mortar, it has greater power and less mobility; its ammunition is heavier; and its adjustment of fire is comparatively slow because of the long time of flight of the projectile at the longer ranges; its rate of fire after adjustment and its other characteristics are approximately the same.

c. Employment.—The mortars can more readily engage targets of opportunity than artillery and are more suitable for use against point targets.

25. ANTITANK GUN.—The 37-mm antitank gun is a flat-trajectory weapon of the field gun type weighing 950 pounds with its carriage. It fires armor-piercing and high-explosive shell. It pierces 1½ inches of armor at 1,000 yards if impact occurs at 90° to the surface or not more than 200 therefrom. It is very accurate and has a rate of fire of from 15 to 20 aimed shots a minute. It is normally drawn by a 4 by 4 half-ton truck and can be moved only for short distances by hand. The primary mission of the 37-mm gun is to furnish antitank defense. In attack, it is also effective against concrete emplacements.

SECTION IV
TOOLS AND OTHER EQUIPMENT

26. INTRENCHING TOOLS.—*a. General.*—The intrenching tool is an important article of equipment of the infantry soldier.

b. Portable.—Infantry soldiers, with a few exceptions, are equipped with some form of portable tool: shovel, pickmattock, hand ax, or wire cutter. The portable tool suffices for digging individual pits and hasty emplacements and clearing fields of fire when heavier tools are not available.

c. Heavy.—Heavy tools are furnished by engineer units and are distributed to the Infantry when required. A set carried on one vehicle is sufficient for an infantry battalion. It includes pick mattocks, shovels, and a supply of axes, saws, large wire cutters, tracing tape, sandbags, and other pioneer equipment.

27. PROTECTION AGAINST CHEMICAL AGENTS.—The gas mask is issued to all individuals. It gives full eye and lung protection against war gases in concentrations likely to be encountered in the field. The diaphragm mask is issued to officers, telephone operators, and others whose duties require audible speech. Protective clothing designed for the protection of the body against gases of the mustard type may be furnished. […]

28. OBSERVATION AND TOPOGRAPHIC EQUIPMENT.—The Infantry is provided with field glasses and telescopes and with simple mapping equipment (compasses, plane tables, sketching cases).

29. SIGNAL COMMUNICATION EQUIPMENT.—*a. Means.*—The normal means of signal communication for the Infantry includes messengers, arm-and-hand signals, sound-and-light signals, the telephone, telegraph, radio, pyrotechnics, panels, and airplane pick-up devices. Other devices may be issued for use in special Situations. […]

b. Codes and ciphers.—Signals transmitted to airplanes by signal panels are prescribed in the air–ground liaison code. The pyrotechnic code is prescribed by the high command and is frequently changed. The division field code is used for condensing messages and maintaining secrecy. It is furnished to message centers of divisions and lower units to include battalions. The Infantry is also provided with a cipher device, the use of-which is explained in FM 24-5.

The .30-cal M1 Garand rifle has attracted many superlatives. Probably the most ringing endorsement came from General George S. Patton—note an easy man to impress—who called the Garand "the greatest battle implement ever devised." The M1 replaced its bolt-action predecessor, the M1903 Springfield, as the standard U.S. service rifle in 1936, being the first universal standard-issue, self-loading army rifle in history. Its chief advantage was its semi-automatic mechanism. The M1-armed infantryman could put down shots as fast as he could pull the trigger, and at least twice as quickly as a soldier armed with a bolt-action rifle (as most of the German infantry were). This facility gave U.S. infantry squads a supreme firepower advantage in small-unit actions. FM 23-5, *U.S. Rifle, Caliber .30, M1*, here describes how to operate the rifle, a process that needed some care if the user wasn't to trap his thumb in the released bolt, resulting in the injury known as "Garand thumb."

From FM 23-5, *U.S. Rifle, Caliber .30, M1* (1942)

SECTION V
OPERATION

20. OBJECT.—This section is designed to give the soldier that instruction necessary for the operation of the rifle.

21. WHEN TAKEN UP.—The operation of the rifle will be taken up at any convenient time after instruction in care and cleaning has been completed.

[…]

23. TO LOAD CARTRIDGE CLIP.—Insert eight rounds in the cartridge clip so that the base of each cartridge is close to the rear wall of the clip and the inner rib of the clip engages the extractor groove in the cartridge. It is immaterial whether the uppermost cartridge of the loaded clip is on the left or right side as the follower slide adjusts itself for either loading. Experience shows, however, that for ease in inserting the clip the soldier prefers to have the uppermost cartridge on the right side of the clip.

24. TO LOAD RIFLE.—*a.* The operation of loading is performed with the piece locked, i.e., with the safety of the piece in its rearmost position except in sustained firing. Hold the rifle at the balance in the left hand. With the forefinger of the right hand, pull the operating rod handle smartly to the rear until the operating rod is caught by the operating rod catch. With the right hand take a fully loaded clip and place it on top of the follower. Place the right side of the right hand against the operating rod handle and with the thumb of the right hand press the clip down into the receiver until it engages the clip latch. Swing the thumb to the right so as to clear the bolt in its forward movement and release the operating rod handle. The closing of the bolt may be assisted by a push forward on the operating rod handle with the heel of the right hand. The technique of loading the rifle properly is readily acquired after performing the operation a few times with dummy cartridges in accordance with these instructions.

b. The loading and reloading of the rifle without hurried movements and consequent fumbling will be demonstrated and taught to all men under instruction.

25. To UNLOAD RIFLE.—*a.* To unload a cartridge from the chamber, hook the right thumb over the operating rod handle, pull and hold the operating rod in the extreme rear position, thus extracting and ejecting the round.

b. To remove the loaded clip from the receiver, hold the rifle with the right hand, thumb on operating rod handle, fingers around the trigger guard. Place the fingers of the left hand over the receiver and press in on the clip latch with the left thumb. The clip will then be ejected upward from the receiver and into the left hand.

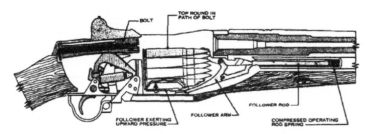

Figure 24. Position of parts when the bolt is in its rearmost position.

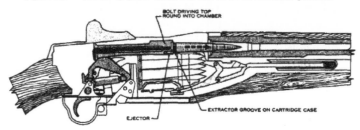

Figure 25. Chambering.

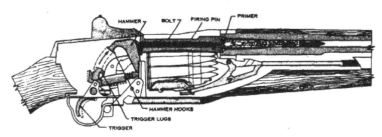

Figure 26. Locking.

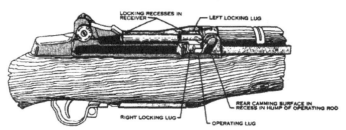

Figure 27. Firing.

Operating cycle of the M1 Garand rifle.

CAUTION: Do not allow the bolt to move forward during the operation as it will push the top cartridge forward and prevent normal ejection of the clip.

c. To close the bolt on an empty chamber and retain the loaded clip in the receiver, press down on the top cartridge in the clip and allow the bolt to slide forward, making sure that it is fully closed.

26. TO OPERATE RIFLE AS SINGLE LOADER.—The receiver being empty, pull the operating rod to the rear until it is caught by the operating rod catch. With the right hand, place one round in the chamber, seating it in place with the thumb. With the right side of the right hand against the operating rod handle and the fingers extended and joined, force the operating rod handle slightly to the rear, depress the follower with the right thumb, and permit the bolt to ride forward about 1 inch over the follower. Then remove the thumb from the follower, release the operating rod handle and push forward on the operating rod handle with the heel of the hand to be certain that the bolt is completely closed. No type of ammunition will be loaded into the receiver except in full clips.

27. TO FIRE RIFLE.—Squeeze the trigger for each shot. When the eighth shot has been fired, the empty clip is automatically ejected and the bolt remains open.

28. TO SET RIFLE AT SAFE.—The loaded rifle will be kept locked until the moment for firing. To make this adjustment set the safety in its rearmost position inside the trigger guard. In this position the trigger cannot be pulled as the upper end of the trigger is blocked from disengaging from the hammer hooks, and the hammer is held in the cocked position by the hook on the safety being engaged with the lug on the left side of the hammer. The rifle may be loaded and operated by hand when locked but cannot be fired. To unlock the rifle set the safety in its foremost position.

29. TO ADJUST REAR SIGHT.—The rear sight is adjusted for range by turning the elevating knob on the left side. This knob has numbered graduations for 200, 400, 600, 800, 1,000, and 1,200 yards of range and index lines between these graduations for 100, 300, 500, 700, 900, and 1,100 yards. Adjustment for windage is made by turning the windage knob on the right. Each windage graduation represents an angular adjustment of 4 minutes. Both elevating and windage knobs are provided with "clicks" which represent approximately 1 minute of angle or 1 inch on the target for each 100 yards of range. Arrows on the knobs indicate the direction in which to turn them to secure corresponding changes in the point of impact of the bullet. Rotation of the elevating knob may be eased by forcing the knob outward (away from receiver) while turning.

30. SAFETY PRECAUTIONS.—The soldier must be impressed with the fact that while any cartridges remain in the receiver, after a round has been fired, the rifle is

ready to fire. The gun is safe only when it is "cleared"; in other words, the gun is never known to be safe when the bolt is closed.

31. TO CLEAR RIFLE.—*a*. To clear rifle, pull the operating rod fully to the rear, extracting and ejecting the cartridge from the chamber. Remove the clip from the magazine as described in paragraph 25 and leave the bolt open.

b. In range firing, whenever firing ceases, execute clear rifle as prescribed above.

The .30-cal Browning M1919A4 was a real workhorse machine gun of the U.S. Army infantry. Firing at a cyclical rate of up to 600rpm from 25-round belts, but fitted with a buttstock for handling in the assault role, it was a true general-purpose machine gun, with an effective range up to 1,500 yards. As well as its use by infantry weapons platoons, it was also found in vehicle-mounted set-ups.

From FM 23-45, *Browning Machine Gun, Caliber .30 HB, M1919A4 Ground* (1940)

SECTION I
DESCRIPTION

1. PRINCIPLE OF OPERATION.—The machine gun, caliber .30, M1919A4, is recoil operated, belt fed, and air cooled. In recoil operation the rearward force of the expanding powder gas (kick) furnishes the operating energy. The moving parts, while locked together at the moment of the explosion, are left free within the receiver to be forced to the rear by the recoil. This movement is controlled by means of various springs, cams, and levers, and is utilized to perform the necessary mechanical operations of unlocking the breech, extraction and ejection of the empty case, and feeding in of the new round, as well as cocking, locking, and firing the mechanism. The receiver mechanism is for all practical purposes the receiver of the Browning machine gun, M1917.

2. COOLING SYSTEM.—The machine gun, caliber .30 M1919A4, is provided with a heavy barrel which is exposed to the air. This factor serves to keep the gun at operating temperatures under normal conditions, i.e., at the rate of about 60 rounds per minute for about 30 minutes.

3. FEED BELT.—Woven fabric belts of a capacity of 150 rounds, equipped with brass strips at each end to facilitate loading, are normally used with the ground light machine gun.

4. MOUNTINGS.

a. The ground light machine gun normally is mounted on the light machine gun tripod M2, a description of which is given in section VI.

b. In motorized or mechanized units, the light machine gun is mounted on vehicular mounts of several types, but a light machine gun tripod M2 is usually carried for each gun to be used when the gun is fired from the ground.

5. GENERAL DATA.—General data for the light machine gun and mount are as follows:

6. SIGHTS.

a. Front.—The front sight consists of a front sight blade, a front side body, a front sight post, and a plunger mechanism. The front sight post pivots on the front sight bearing screw when folded for convenience in packing. The plunger mechanism provides a locking device to keep the front sight post in its upright position when the gun is being fired. The front sight is attached to the front end of the receiver by means of a screw. The height of the front sight is such that when the rear sight slide is set at an elevation a bullet fired from the gun will strike a target at a distance corresponding to the elevation set on the rear sight.

b. Rear.—

(1) The rear sight is of conventional type. It consists of a rear sight leaf, carrying a peep in the slide mounting, pivoted on the rear sight base, and adjustable for windage. The rear sight base mounts the rear sight leaf and rear sight leaf spring. It is secured to the left side plate of the receiver by three screws in the flange of the base.

(2) The rear sight leaf is graduated for elevation in 100 yard divisions up to 2,400 yards. The peep of the rear sight slide is 0.081 inch in diameter. Motion of the rear sight slide is accomplished by rotation of the elevating screw knob. This elevating screw mechanism is equipped with a mil click device which may be used in conjunction with a mil scale engraved on the left side of the rear sight leaf to measure or establish angles of elevation in mils.

(3) The windage screw mechanism also incorporates a mil click device. Adjustment of the rear sight leaf in windage is accomplished by rotation of the windage screw knob. Amount of motion permitted is 10 mils right or left from zero.

(4) The sight radius is 13.94 inches.

7. PINTLE.—The pintle of the light machine gun (ground), although technically not a part of the gun, is permanently assembled thereto by a bolt through the trunnions of the pintle and the trunnion hole of the receiver of the gun. Failure to keep this bolt tight will result in inaccuracy of fire. This pintle is tapered and mates with the corresponding tapered pintle bushing of the tripod mount M2 head. This

M1919A4 machine gun and its two-man crew.

tapered pintle thus serves as a tight wearing union between the receiver of the gun and its mounting. The pintle is secured in its mounting by the engagement of a spring actuated pintle latch of the mounting in a corresponding annular groove of the pintle.

8. ELEVATING AND TRAVERSING MECHANISM.

a. As with the pintle, the elevating and traversing mechanism is not technically a part of the gun. However, the elevating and traversing mechanism is permanently secured to the receiver of the gun by a bolt through the head of this mechanism and the elevating bracket of the gun. In guns of new manufacture, the elevating bracket is integral with the bottom plate.

b. The elevating and traversing mechanism, when used with the tripod M2, consists of an upper elevating screw; a lower elevating screw; an elevating handwheel assembly secured to the head of the lower elevating screw; a housing mating with the lower elevating screw; a traversing block mounted by a swivel joint to the lower elevating screw housing.

(1) The upper elevating screw terminates at its upper end in an offset head which incorporates a recess for the bolt which assembles the entire elevating and traversing mechanism to the gun. The mechanism is properly assembled to the gun when the offset head points to the rear, thus permitting the mechanism to be folded to the rear and seated in its recess in the duralumin grip. The inner elevating screw is externally threaded to mate with the internal threads of the lower elevating screw. It is equipped with a longitudinal slot in which is seated an engraved scale. This scale is utilized to indicate plus or minus increments of elevation given the mounted gun. It is subdivided into 50-mil graduations and is read by noting the position of the upper edge of the traversing bar and the traversing slide lock lever preferably engaged. (When firing on rapidly moving ground targets, the traversing clamp is not engaged, although the traversing block must be retained in firm contact with the traversing bar.)

(2) Movement of the light machine gun in traverse, when mounted on the tripod M2, is accomplished by moving the gun right or left as desired, the traversing clamp being disengaged from the traversing bar but the traversing block remaining in firm contact with the traversing bar.

In effect, mortars provided the infantry with their own portable artillery, which could be set up in minutes and had a rate of fire significantly ahead of that of heavier tube artillery. Typically, a 60mm mortar would engage targets from a protected position about 500 yards behind the combat frontline, firing at visually identified targets. The 81mm mortar would be further back, engaging either pre-registered targets or targets radioed in by forward observers. But in emergencies, mortars could hit targets of opportunity at far closer ranges, by virtue of their high launch trajectory, which also made them useful in woodland combat, where they could fire up through gaps in the trees.

The following manual gives the technical details of both of the main types of mortar used by the infantry. It then goes on to talk about U.S. hand grenades, their types and purpose. Hand grenades do not deliver the powerful explosions as seen in many Hollywood films, but their fragmentation effect had exceptional real-world utility for clearing rooms, bunkers, trenches, and other field positions. They were certainly used in huge volumes—the U.S. manufactured more than 50 million of them during the war.

From *Weapon and Ammunition Technical Manual, Infantry Regiment, Parachute* (1944)

60 MM MORTAR, M2, MOUNT, M2

The 60 mm Mortar, M2, is of French origin, developed by the Edgar Brandt Company, but manufactured in the United States under rights purchased from the Brandt organization. Its design has been altered and improved to conform to our standards. In addition to its normal function, it is now utilized as a projector for the illuminating shell, M83, employed to disclose aerial targets at night.

MORTAR, M2—The mortar consists of the barrel, base cap and firing pin. The base cap, ending in a spherical projection which fits into a socket in the base plate, is screwed to the breech end of the smooth-bored barrel. The firing pin fits in the base cap, which is bored and threaded axially to receive it.

MOUNT, M2—The bipod mount comprises the leg, elevating mechanism and traversing mechanism assemblies. The leg assembly consists of two tubular steel legs connected by a clevis joint attached to the elevating screw guide tube. Spread of the legs is limited by the clevis joint, which is provided with a spring latch to lock the legs in the open position. The legs terminate in spiked feet. The left leg has a cross-leveling mechanism consisting of a sliding bracket connected by a link to the elevating screw guide tube. The elevating mechanism assembly consists mainly of an elevating screw nut which moves vertically on a screw within a guide tube, the elevating screw being actuated by a crank attached to its lower end. The traversing mechanism consists of a horizontal screw operating in a yoke and actuated by a traversing handwheel. The sight bracket fits in a dovetail slot provided in the yoke. The barrel is clamped to the bipod by means of a clamping collar and saddle, shock absorbers being used to stabilize the mortar and mount during firing. The base plate consists of a pressed steel body to which are welded a series of ribs and braces, a front flange and a socket. A locking lever fastens the spherical projection of the base cap in the socket.

Sighting and Fire Control Equipment

Sight (Collimator), M4

Ammunition

Projectile and propelling charge are in one unit constituting a complete round. The shell is furnished with stabilizing fins and a nose fuse. Propelling charges are divided into parts to provide for zone firing.

CHARACTERISTICS

MORTAR, M2

Weight of Mortar, M2, and Mount, MP............................42.0 lb.
Weight of mortar..12.8 lb.
Overall length of mortar...8.6 ins.
Diameter of bore..2.36 ins.
Rate of fire, maximum..30 to 35 rds./min.
Rate of fire, normal...18 rds./min.

MOUNT, M2

Weight of mount..29.2 lb.
Weight of bipod...16.4 lb.
Weight of base plate..2.8 lb.
Elevations, approximate...40° to 85°
    Mortar clamp position A...40° to 65°
    Mortar clamp position B...45° to 70°
    Mortar clamp position C...50° to 85°
Maximum traverse, right...70 mils.
Maximum traverse, left..70 mils.

AMMUNITION

Shell	Range, Approximate
H.E., M49A2	100 to 1,985 yds.
Illumination, M83	
Training, M69	

81 MM MORTAR, M1, MOUNT, M1

During the first World War, the standard mortar adopted by the U. S. Army for infantry use as an indirect fire weapon was the British 3" Stokes trench mortar, Mk. 1. Designs for a new mortar were started in 1920, but were abandoned in favor of attempts to improve bomb vanes in an effort to attain greater accuracy. While these tests were under way, the French firm of Edgar Brandt succeeded in developing a refined version of the Stokes mortar, together with suitable ammunition, which satisfied the requirements of the 17. S. War Department. After tests of the Stokes–Brandt mortar and mount were completed successfully by the Ordnance Department, and the using arms, manufacturing rights were purchased from the Brandt Company. The 81 mm Mortar, M1, has a heavier barrel than the Stokes, Mk. 1, and a heavier base plate of new design. It also has a greater range and a higher rate of fire.

MORTAR, M1—The complete weapon consists of a barrel, bipod and base plate. The barrel is demountable from the bipod to form one load, while the bipod and base plate comprise two loads. Each load is light enough to be carried by one man. The smooth-bore muzzle-loading barrel is a seamless drawn-steel tube fitted at the breech end with a base cap within which is secured a firing pin protruding into the barrel.

MOUNT, M1—The mount consists of a base plate and a tubular steel bipod formed by two legs attached to a center trunnion by means of a compass joint. The left leg carries a cross-leveling mechanism which consists of a sliding bracket connected with the guide tube by a connecting rod. The mortar clamp, in two sections, clamps the barrel to the bipod and can be adjusted to three positions on the barrel. The base plate is a rectangular pressed steel body to which are welded a series of ribs and braces, a front flange, three loops, two handle plates and a socket for the spherical end of the tube base cap.

Sighting and Fire Control Equipment

Each mortar is equipped with a sight which includes a collimator, elevating and lateral deflection mechanisms, and longitudinal and cross-levels. The sight mechanism, supported by a bracket fitted into the mortar yoke, provides accurate laying for elevation and deflection. Sight, M4, and Aiming Posts, M7, 118 and M9, are used with the 81 mm mortar.

An 81mm mortar team of the 504th Parachute Infantry Regiment, Italy, 1943.

Transportation

The 81 mm mortar can be carried by two men or can be transported on Hand Cart, M6A1. It is also part of the armament of the Half Track 81 mm Mortar Carrier, M4.

Ammunition

Stabilization in flight is obtained by fins on the shell which cause the projectile to strike nose first. A point detonating impact type of fuse is fitted to the nose of the shell. The propelling charge attached to the base end of the projectile consists of an ignition cartridge and propellant increment. The increments of the charge arc removable to provide for zone firing.

CHARACTERISTICS

MORTAR, M1

Weight of Mortar, M1, and Mount, M1...........................136.0 lb.
Weight of mortar..44.5 lb.
Overall length of mortar...49.5 ins.
Diameter of bore...3.2 ins.
Rate of fire, maximum..30 to 35 rds./min.
Rate of fire, normal..18 rds./min.

MOUNT, M1

Weight of mount...91.5 lb.
Weight of bipod..46.5 lb.
Weight of base plate..45.0 lb.
Elevations, approximate..40º to 85º
Mortar clamp position A...40º to 70º
Mortar clamp position B...50º to 80º
Mortar clamp position C...55º to 85º
Maximum traverse, right...65 mils.
Maximum traverse, left...65 mils.

AMMUNITION

Weight	Ranges, Approximate
H.E. shell,	M43A1, 6.87 lb.........100 to 3,290 yds.
	M36, 10.62 lb............300 to 2,558 yds.
Chemical shell, M57,10.75 lb..............……................300 to 2,470 yds.	

[…]

HAND GRENADES
GRENADE, HAND, FRAGMENTATION, MK. IIA1
GRENADE, HAND, OFFENSIVE, MK. IIIA1
GRENADE, HAND, PRACTICE, MK. II
GRENADE, HAND, TRAINING, MK. IA1

TYPES

1. **FRAGMENTATION HAND GRENADES**—containing a high-explosive charge in a metallic body which is shattered by the explosion of the charge.

2. **OFFENSIVE HAND GRENADES**—containing a high-explosive charge in a paper body, designed for demolition or lethal shock effect.

3. **CHEMICAL HAND GRENADES**—containing a chemical agent which produces a toxic or irritant effect, a screening smoke, incendiary action or any combination of these actions.

4. **PRACTICE HAND GRENADES**—containing a reduced charge; simulate fragmentation grenades.

5. **TRAINING HAND GRENADES**—used in training troops; do not contain explosives or chemicals. The filler in a grenade may be a powerful explosive, a gas, a smoke-producing or an incendiary agent. The filler in fragmentation grenades is either TNT (trinitrotoluene) or EC Blank Fire Smoke-less Powder. The latter is used in loading blank ammunition for small arms weapons.

FILLERS—EC powder is less powerful than TNT and usually is exploded by all igniting rather than a detonating agent. Grenades loaded with EC powder are issued fuzed and ready for use. They are not susceptible to mass detonation.

The standard filler for offensive grenades is pressed TNT.

Fillers in chemical grenades consist of various chemical mixtures and solutions. The manufacturing, storage and issue of Chemical Grenades is a function of the Chemical Warfare Service.

Practice Grenades contain a small amount of black powder and are designed to give an indicating puff of smoke when the igniting type fuze functions.

TIME AND AUTOMATIC FUZES—The fuze is the device which causes the grenade to function. All standard hand grenade fuzes (including most of the chemical hand grenade fuzes) are Time and Automatic types. A "time" fuze fires the grenade after a lapse of time and not upon percussion or impact. Grenades which contain an "automatic" fuze function automatically as soon as the grenade leaves the hand, provided the safety pin has been removed and the safety lever held close to the body of the grenade prior to throwing. This lever provides a safety feature by eliminating the necessity of manually starting the fuze action before the grenade is thrown toward the target.

FUZE CLASSIFICATION—Hand grenade fuzes are either detonating or igniting types.

A detonating fuze is used when shock is necessary to initiate the action of the explosive filler.

Igniting fuzes are used when the filler is one which requires heat initiation. This type of fuze will ignite the filler as though it had been lighted by a match.

All detonating and igniting hand grenade fuzes have the same general form and appearance. The fuze assembly consists primarily of a fuze body, having a threaded portion to permit insertion into the grenade body, a safety lever which restrains a striker, a safety pin to hold the lever in place, and a deep cup which is crimped to the lower portion of the fuze body and extends inside the grenade body when the fuze is assembled. The compound in the cup determines whether the final action of the fuze will be one of detonation or ignition.

OPERATION—The safety device is a cotter pin with ring attached which enables it to be withdrawn easily. One end of the safety lever covers the top of the fuze body, sealing it against foreign bodies, and hooks over a lip in the fuze body. The other end of the safety lever extends downward and follows the contour of the grenade.

A grenade should be held with the safety lever pressed close to the grenade body by the palm of the hand. The thrower must take every precaution after withdrawing the safety pin, not to release his grip on the safety lever.

When the grenade is thrown, the safety lever is detached by the release of the striker spring and the impact of the striker. When no longer restrained by the lever, the striker rotates about a hinge pin and strikes a primer in the upper part of the fuze body.

The primer is a center-fire type similar to a shotgun shell primer. The flame from the primer charge ignites a delay charge which in the 1M6A3 and M10A3 fuzes consists of a powder column compressed in a lead tube. The burning time varies from 4.0 to 5.0 seconds.

The delay charge ignites a black powder igniting charge in the M10A3 fuze and a tetryl detonator in the M6A3 fuze. The igniter or detonator initiates the filler charge. The total burning time of the assembly is the same as the fuze, namely from 4.0 to 5.0 sec.

GRENADE, HAND, FRAGMENTATION, MK. IIA1— STANDARD—
The body of this grenade is made of cast-iron and is about the size of a large lemon. The outside surface is deeply serrated horizontally and vertically to assist in producing

uniform fragments when the grenade explodes. The bursting charge is 0.74 ounce of EC Black Fire Powder initiated by the M10A3 igniting fuze. The grenade loaded and fuzed weighs 21 ounces. The bursting radius is 30 yards.

GRENADE, HAND, OFFENSIVE, MK. IIIA1—LIMITED STANDARD—This grenade consists of a sheet-metal top, threaded to receive the detonating fuze, M6A3, and a body of laminated cartridge paper which contains the high explosive TNT charge. This grenade is for demolition. It may be used in the open more safely than the fragmentation grenade because there is no marked fragmentation. The grenade bodies and fuzes are shipped separately. The loaded and fuzed Mk. IIIA1 grenade weighs 14 ounces, 6.83 ounces of which is the TNT charge.

GRENADE, HAND, PRACTICE, MK. II—STANDARD—This is a standard practice grenade and is equipped with the igniting fuze, M10A3. The grenade is loaded with a small charge of black powder in a cloth bag. The grenade when fuzed weighs 20.5 ounces.

GRENADE, HAND, TRAINING, MK. IAl—STANDARD—This grenade is the current standard for practice and training. It consists of a one piece cast-iron body in the shape of a Mk. II fuzed fragmentation grenade and a removable safety pin and ring. It is inert. The grenade weighs 22 ounces, 1 ounce more than the Mk. II.

The 2.36in A.T. Rocket Launcher is far better known to history as the "bazooka," a nickname deriving from the weapon's resemblance to a weird "bazooka" musical instrument developed by the comedian Bob Burns during the 1930s. It was a recoilless shoulder-launched weapon firing a shaped-charge warhead that could penetrate 3–4in of armor, depending on the variant. It entered service in 1942 as the M1, then came the improved M1A1 in 1943, followed by the more powerful M9 and M9A1 in 1943–44. The bazooka's value lay not just in its ability to puncture enemy armor, which it did, but also for destroying enemy bunkers and protected positions.

From TM 9-294, *2.36-inch A.T. Rocket Launcher M1A1* **(1943)**

Section I
INTRODUCTION

1. SCOPE.

a. This manual is published for the information and guidance of personnel charged with the operation and maintenance of the 2.36-inch AT Rocket Launcher M1A1. It contains information required by the using arms to identify, use, care, and preserve the materiel and the ammunition used therewith. In addition, it contains information required by ordnance personnel for the maintenance and repair of the materiel.

2. CHARACTERISTICS.

a. The 2.36-inch AT Rocket Launcher M1A1 is an electrically operated weapon of the open tube type. It is fired from the shoulder in the standing, kneeling, sitting, or prone positions. It is used to launch high-explosive rockets against tanks, armored vehicles, pill boxes, and emplacements. The rockets weigh approximately 3½ pounds and are capable of penetrating heavy armor at angles of impact up to 30 degrees. The weapon can be aimed up to distances of 300 yards. Greater ranges may be obtained by estimating the angle of elevation. The maximum range is 700 yards.

3. DATA.

Length of launcher (approx.)	54.5 in.
Weight of launcher (approx.)	13.26 lb
Internal diameter	2.37 in.
Length of rocket	21.6 in.
Weight of rocket	3.5 lb
Muzzle velocity	265 ft per sec

4. PRECAUTIONS.

a. Do not expose rockets to the sun except when immediately ready to load. Store rockets in their containers in shaded places.

b. Do not allow a rocket to remain in a hot launcher prior to firing.

c. Rockets as shipped contain a small cardboard plug cemented over the nozzle in the forward end of the fin assembly. This prevents entry of moisture or dirt into the propellent charge during storage and handling. Do not use any rocket with a missing cardboard plug. Do not remove the plug.

d. Since the fuze of the rocket is quite sensitive, it is important that the rocket be handled carefully after removal of the safety pin, and that it not be dropped. A fall on its nose, after removal of the safety wire, will cause detonation.

e. The burning time of the propellant is approximately 0.02 to 0.03 seconds, and combustion is complete before the rocket leaves the muzzle, hence there is no flash. Occasionally, however, the burning may, for some reason, be retarded, creating a backflash as the rocket leaves the muzzle. This occurs during cold weather but may also occur at other times. The firer should be protected against this by gloves or cloth wrapped around the hands, goggles, or other protective equipment, such as a gas mask. This precaution is especially important in cold climates or when no flash deflector is available. It is also recommended that both the firer and the loader wear steel helmets when using the launcher.

f. The launcher may be fired from the shoulder in the standing, kneeling, sitting, or prone positions. If fired from the prone position, the body should be at an angle of at least 45 degrees to the direction of fire so as to avoid injury from the back blast of the rocket.

A U.S. soldier training with an M1 "bazooka."

g. In using the launcher, it is essential that no personnel, or inflammable material be directly behind the launcher within a distance of 20 feet.

h. Never stand in or near the rear of the launcher while it is being fired because the hot gases can inflict serious burns. When firing from trenches or fox holes, clearance should be provided so that back blast is not deflected against personnel.

i. At temperatures below 14 F, the dry cells become too weak to fire this weapon. When used at low temperatures, batteries should be removed from the launcher and kept warm until just before firing. Carrying the batteries in inner pockets in cold climates will keep them sufficiently warm. The spare batteries can be carried in the pockets and switched with the cold ones every half hour.

j. The rockets should not be fired at temperatures below zero F nor above 120 F.

Section II
DESCRIPTION AND FUNCTIONING

5. DESCRIPTION.

a. The launcher is essentially a long open barrel with a stock which houses the electrical firing mechanism. The tube is approximately 54 inches long and has a smooth bore.

b. The launcher has a front and rear sight, both of which are fixed to the barrel on the left side. The rear sight is of the peep type. The front sight consists of three studs which are used for ranges of 100, 200, and 300 yards. Intermediate or greater ranges, lead, and windage must be estimated by the firer.

c. Ahead of the front sight is assembled a flash deflector. The deflector is a conical wire screen with a mounting clamp. It is secured to the tube by the deflector screw and nut. When properly assembled, the mounting clamp of the deflector overlaps the muzzle end of the launcher. The function of the deflector is to deflect occasional particles of unburned powder which might impinge upon the firer's face.

d. The hand grip consists of the left and right trigger grips attached to the trigger support. The trigger support accommodates the trigger guard, trigger, and the lower and upper trigger switch contacts. The trigger is pinned at its upper end to the trigger support and is free to pivot. When the trigger is squeezed, it presses the bar contact against the lower trigger switch contact to complete the electric circuit. When the pressure on the trigger is released, the trigger spring forces the trigger to the forward position so as to break the electric circuit.

e. The stock has a narrow vertical slot by means of which it slips over the stock support to which it is attached by screws. In the bottom of the stock there are two vertical cylindrical compartments for accommodating four batteries. The two batteries in the rear compartment are in actual use; the two batteries in the front compartment are spares. On the left side of the stock is a small electric lamp for testing the electric circuit and battery. The lamp is connected in parallel with the firing mechanism and it lights when the trigger is squeezed, regardless of whether a rocket is in the launcher or not. A spare lamp is carried in a circular compartment on the right side of the stock under the circuit indicator cover. The bottom of the stock is fitted with a hasp assembly which keeps the batteries in position and completes the electric circuit. The hasp assembly is kept closed by a spring actuated hasp catch which engages the stock pin. The battery spring contacts the batteries and is connected by wire to the stock support to complete the electric circuit.

f. The face guard is on the barrel above the stock. The guard serves to protect the firer's face from the heat in the tube. The guard is pressed on to the barrel and is held in position by its tension.

g. The portion of the barrel from the rear of the stock to the insulated contact spring is wound with bracing wire. The contact springs serve as connecting points for the contact wire leading from the rocket. In this manner, the circuit is completed. At the rear of the barrel is a spring actuated tail latch assembly. The function of the latch is to engage notches on the tail of the rocket and hold it in position for firing. The breech guard at the breech end of the barrel facilitates loading of the rocket, protects the tail latch assembly, prevents distortion of the end of the barrel, and prevents entry of dirt and foreign material when the end of launcher rests on the ground.

h. When the 2.36-inch AT Rocket Launcher M1A1 is issued, it is equipped with a battery designated as the Eveready 791-A, to provide current for operating the firing mechanism. This battery consists of two dry cell batteries of the Eveready No. BA-42 type, size C, which are jointed together and placed in a cardboard container. When replacement is necessary and a battery of the original type cannot be supplied by ordnance personnel, two separate cells of the battery BA-42 type will be used. These cells are a standard Signal Corps item which are readily available in the field. Each is 15/16 inch in diameter and 1 15/16 inches in over-all length.

6. FUNCTIONING.

a. When the trigger is squeezed, it forces the bar contact against the lower trigger switch contact to complete the circuit.

b. The passage of the electric current through the rocket sets off an electric igniter in the rocket which in turn ignites the propelling charge. Rearward escape of the powder gases through a jet forces the rocket out of the barrel with a muzzle velocity of about 265 feet per second. Propulsion of the rocket is by jet action of the propellent powder and hence there is no recoil.

Section III
OPERATION

7. PRECAUTION.

a. During the operations of loading, sighting, and firing, the loader should at no time stand directly behind the launcher.

b. See other precautions in paragraph 4.

8. LOADING.

a. The firer places the launcher on his right shoulder and aims at the target. The firer tests the circuit by squeezing the trigger several times. The light bulb should light only when the trigger is squeezed.

b. The firer makes certain that the light is out and he must not squeeze the trigger while the rocket is being loaded into the launcher.

c. The loader grasps the rocket by the tube and inserts the high-explosive head into the launcher barrel, at the same time raising the tail latch clear of the rocket.

d. Having inserted the head of the rocket into the launcher, the loader then releases the tail latch and removes the safety pin from the fuze.

e. The loader again raises the tail latch and carefully pushes the rocket into the launcher until the tail latch engages a notch on the tail fins.

f. The loader pulls the end of the contact wire of the fin, pulls the wire straight back to uncoil it, and then engages the uninsulated portion of the wire in any of the coils of either of the contact springs. The launcher is ready to be fired.

9. SIGHTING.

a. The firer estimates distances to target and picks proper stud on front sight for aiming. He then sights at target through rear sight by centering stud in peep of sight. The firer estimates intermediate or greater ranges, lead, and windage.

10. FIRING.

a. Firing. To fire the launcher, the firer squeezes the trigger and releases it.

b. Firing Positions. The launcher can be fired in the standing, kneeling, sitting, or prone positions.

1. UNLOADING.

a. To unload the launcher, the loader removes the wire from the contact spring, raises the tail latch, and carefully withdraws rocket until safety pin can be reinserted. He then inserts safety pin and removes rocket completely from the launcher. He coils and places the contact wire between the fins, and repacks the rocket.

CHAPTER 4
COMBAT DOCTRINE

By World War II, infantry combat doctrine on all sides was largely bifurcated into offensive tactics—i.e. how to make an attack on an enemy position—and how to conduct a defense. There were, of course, specialist sub-sections of tactics, such as how to perform reconnaissance and undertake patrols, or how to fight enemy armor, but both of these sections still orbited around the principles of attack and defense. For offensive action, the classic goals were either to push the enemy back through a direct frontal assault, destabilize the enemy position through attacks on weaker flanks or via encirclement, make a focused penetration at one point, or simply pound it into destruction with firepower (the latter rarely worked perfectly). On the defense, the tactics were intended to prevent the enemy from making his own flanking or encircling attacks, while also inflicting such significant losses that the enemy commanders are compelled to call the effort off.

Each infantry unit and formation had its own offensive and defensive principles, based on the size of the unit and the weapons at its disposal. A U.S. Army infantry battalion, for example, was capable of launching an attack across a frontage of 500–1,000 yards, with support from its heavy weapons company. In the following extract from FM 7-10, *Rifle Company, Rifle Regiment*, however, we concentrate on the smallest scale of tactical decision-making, at rifle squad level. This analysis is not divorced from larger unit maneuvers, as ultimately any attack was composed of the actions of the minor units and even those of individuals. Only when acting as a unified whole, tactically and morally, was a large unit capable of battle-winning results.

From FM 7-10, *Rifle Company, Rifle Regiment* **(1942)**

CHAPTER 6
RIFLE SQUAD

SECTION I
GENERAL

133. COMPOSITION.—The rifle squad consists of a sergeant (squad leader), a corporal (assistant squad leader and antitank rifle grenadier), an automatic rifle team (automatic rifleman, assistant automatic rifleman, and ammunition bearer), and seven riflemen, two of whom are designated as scouts.

134. DUTIES OF LEADERS.—*a.* The squad leader is responsible for the discipline, appearance, training, control, and conduct of his squad. He leads it in combat. Under the platoon leader's direction, the squad leader arranges for feeding his men, enforces proper observance of rules of personal hygiene and sanitation, requires that weapons and equipment be kept clean and in serviceable condition, and checks and reports on the ammunition supply within the squad. His squad must be trained to use and care for its weapons, to move and fight efficiently as individuals, and function effectively as a part of the military team.

b. The assistant squad leader performs duties assigned by the squad leader and takes command of the squad in his absence. He carries the antitank rifle and, during a tank attack, engages with antitank rifle grenades any hostile tanks within range. The squad leader may designate him to command a portion of the squad, to act as observer, or to supervise replenishment of ammunition.

135. TARGET DESIGNATION.—Battlefield targets are generally indistinct. They must be designated with such accuracy and simplicity as to be unmistakable. Squad leaders and other members of the squad are trained to designate the location and extent of such targets.

136. FIRE CONTROL.—*a.* Fire control implies the ability of the squad leader to open fire when he desires, adjust the fire of his squad upon the target, shift the fire of all or part of the squad from one target to another, regulate the rate of fire, and cease firing at will.

b. The squad leader announces the range, designates the target, and gives the command for opening fire. In combat, he controls the fire as long as possible by employing signals or by requiring skirmishers to transmit oral orders along the front of the squad. He concentrates the fire of the squad on the assigned target. On orders of the platoon leader, or on his own initiative, he shifts the fire of all or part of his squad to new targets.

137. FIRE DISCIPLINE.—Fire discipline in the rifle squad is maintained by careful observance of instructions relative to the use of its weapons and exact execution of orders. It requires care in sight setting, aim, and trigger squeeze; close attention to the squad leader; and cessation or change of rate of fire on the squad leader's order or signal. Fire discipline also requires that upon release of fire control by the squad leader to individual skirmishers, each member of the squad acts on his own initiative, selects his target, estimates the range, opens and ceases fire in accordance with the situation, and conserves his ammunition.

138. RANGE.—Ranges can be determined most accurately by sighting shots where the strike of bullets can be observed, or when tracer ammunition is used. Estimation of ranges by eye enables a squad to place surprise fire on the target. All personnel must be trained to estimate ranges by eye.

139. AMMUNITION SUPPLY.—*a.* Each member of the squad habitually carries an initial supply of ammunition on his person; in addition, the assistant automatic rifleman and the ammunition bearer also carry ammunition for the automatic rifle. Similarly, the assistant squad leader carries some rifle ammunition as well as several antitank rifle grenades. Prior to entry into combat, hand grenades and an additional supply of ammunition are issued to all members of the squad. [...]

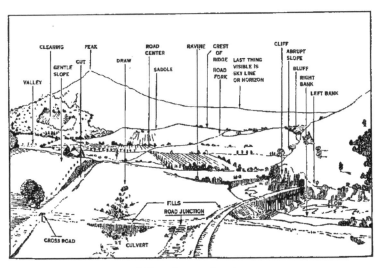

Military features of terrain.

b. During combat the squad leader requests the platoon leader to replenish ammunition and insures that all unexpended ammunition on casualties is secured by members of his squad.

SECTION II
ATTACK

140. FIRE ORDERS.—*a.* The details included in fire orders are dependent upon the time available, cover, and character of the target.

(1) If the target is at close range and unmistakable, fire orders may be limited to the command "commence firing."

(2) Detailed fire orders are not practicable when the squad occupies an exposed position, and fire control must be released to the individual skirmishers.

(3) Whenever practicable, preliminary fire orders are issued under cover before the skirmishers occupy firing positions. When the target cannot be easily identified, the squad leader will have the men creep or crawl sufficiently close to the crest or other mask to see the foreground. He completes the fire order when the men have signified recognition (signal "ready").

[…]

142. APPROACH MARCH.—*a. Dispositions*—When the platoon leaves the route column to take up the approach march the squad marches with the platoon as ordered by the platoon leader. The squad dispositions (formations) are squad column, skirmishers, skirmishers right (left), and squad wedge. The initial (first) formation may be prescribed by the platoon leader; thereafter a squad leader changes the disposition of his squad to meet changes in the situation and terrain. In selecting a formation, the squad leader considers the necessity of employing his weapons promptly, of presenting a poor target to the enemy, and of retaining control of his squad.

(1) "Squad column" is vulnerable to hostile fire from the front and requires a change of formation to permit the employment of all the squad's weapons to the front, but is easily controlled and maneuvered. It is suitable for crossing areas exposed to artillery fire, for utilizing narrow covered routes, and for movement in woods, fog, smoke, and darkness. It facilitates immediate action toward the flanks. The automatic rifleman is posted close to the squad leader near the head of the column. A squad column does not usually exceed 60 paces in depth.

(2) "As skirmishers" is less vulnerable to hostile fire from the front, and enables the squad to employ its weapons to the front without change of formation; but it is more difficult to control than squad column. It is adapted to rapid dashes across open spaces, particularly shelled areas. When the squad is deployed in skirmish line its front ordinarily should not exceed 60 paces.

(3) "Squad wedge" combines most of the advantages, with few of the disadvantages, of the other two dispositions. It is especially adapted to situations when readiness for action in any direction is required; it is frequently used when emerging from cover or from a defile. It is also adapted to take best advantage of cover on broken ground and for traversing zones near the enemy but beyond effective rifle range of known hostile positions.

b. Passing through long-range fire.—When the enemy is covering a zone across the line of advance with long-range machine-gun or artillery fire (interdiction fire), the squad frequently crosses short stretches of such exposed terrain by successive movement of individuals. This action is taken by the squad leader, upon his own initiative or when directed by his platoon leader. Individuals do not stop until they have passed through the area covered by fire; this is particularly important when crossing crests or passing through defiles. The squad leader moves across the area first and reforms his squad beyond the area as the men come through.

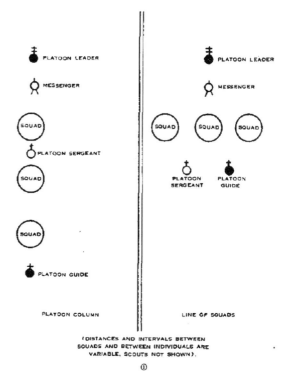

Rifle platoon formations in approach march.

c. Position and duties of leaders.— (1) *Squad leader.*—During the approach march the position of the squad leader is at the head of, or in advance of, his squad. He regulates his advance on the base squad or, being in command of the base squad, advances as directed by the platoon leader. He studies the ground to the front to choose the best route and to control and regulate the movement of his squad. He decreases distances and intervals between individuals as conditions of visibility become poor. He, or a member of the squad designated by him, maintains the prescribed direction. He makes minor detours to take advantage of better routes of advance.

(2) *Assistant squad leader.*—The assistant squad leader is usually posted in rear of the squad to prevent straggling, to prevent elongation or closing up of the squad, and to insure its orderly advance. During a hostile tank attack he takes position where he can best engage the hostile tanks with his antitank rifle grenades.

d. Duties of scouts.— (1) When it is not preceded by friendly troops within view, a rifle platoon in the attacking echelon of a leading company is preceded by its scouts. The scouts operate under control of the platoon leader. Deployed in pairs at wide and irregular intervals, they move out boldly to the front to reconnoiter successive positions (objectives) along the route of advance, and seek to force enemy riflemen and machine guns to disclose their position. One member of each pair watches for signals from the platoon leader. They take advantage of cover without delaying their advance, and cross exposed ground at a run. Their distance in front of the platoon is governed by orders of the platoon leader and varies with the ground and with the probable position of the enemy. One moment they may be 500 yards ahead; at another time they may be absorbed within their units. In approaching houses, natural defiles, and villages, one scout of each pair covers the movement and reconnaissance of the other.

(2) When scouts reach woods, one scout of each pair reconnoiters within the woods for a short distance while the other covers his movement. As soon as the leading scout determines that the edge of the woods is free of the enemy he returns within view and signals "forward." The second scout repeats this signal to the platoon leader. Both scouts then enter the woods and maintain observation toward the enemy until the platoon comes up. Scouts passing through woods ahead of their platoon keep within sight of each other. If an obstacle is encountered, they reconnoiter to the front and flanks. When advancing along a road or path, scouts reconnoiter well to the flanks before signaling "forward" to the platoon. Scouts halt at the far edge of a woods until the platoon leader arrives; he then gives them further directions. When sent ahead to reconnoiter dangerous points, they signal back whether conditions indicate that the platoon halt, continue to march, or quickly rush across the area. They are continually on the lookout for signals from the rear.

(3) If the enemy opens fire, the scouts stop, seek cover, and try to determine the enemy's position. When the enemy position is located, one scout of each pair crawls to the best nearby firing position and opens fire with tracer ammunition to indicate the target. The second scout observes and orders necessary changes in range. When adjustment of fire is completed, he also opens fire. If the scouts have no tracer ammunition, one opens fire and the other points out the target to the platoon leader.

e. Action when scouts are fired on.—When the scouts are halted by fire, the squad leader immediately gets the squad under cover, studies the terrain for covered routes forward, and watches the platoon leader for orders. The squad leader may be directed to reform his squad on the line of scouts and open the fire fight, or to move his squad to some other firing position from which he can more effectively engage the enemy. Avoiding as much as practicable the hostile fire holding up the scouts, the squad leader advances his squad to the firing position by—

(1) *Infiltration of individuals or groups of individuals.*—Where there is little cover or concealment and the area between the firing position and the squad is under enemy observation or fire, the advance is continued by sending forward individuals or groups of two or three men at a time.

(2) *Rushes.*—When the enemy fire permits, and the distance to be covered is short, the squad is moved forward by rushes. Otherwise it is preferable to crawl or creep.

(3) *Using covered route of approach.*—The squad advances as a unit when there is a covered route to the position. The usual formation is either squad column or wedge. The squad leader issues the fire order under cover, has the men creep or crawl to their firing positions, and then open a surprise volume of accurate fire.

f. Fire distribution.—Each member of the squad fires his first shot on that portion of the target corresponding generally to his position in the squad. He then distributes his next shots to the right and left of his first shot, covering that part of the target on which he can deliver accurate fire without having to change position. The amount of the target which one man can cover will depend upon the range and the position of the firer. Frequently each man will be able to cover the entire target with accurate fire; this should be done whenever possible. Fire is not limited to points within the target known to contain an enemy; on the contrary, all men space their shots so that no portion of the target remains unhit. Automatic riflemen fire bursts of about five rounds at the slow cyclic rate (in about 1 second). This method of fire distribution is employed without command. The squad leader observes the fire to insure that the entire target is kept under fire. If other targets appear, he announces such changes in fire distribution as are necessary.

143. PREPARATIONS FOR COORDINATED ATTACK.— *a. Assembly areas.*—(1) Unless the squad, during the approach march, is part of a leading platoon and becomes engaged with the enemy as described in paragraph 106e, it usually is directed to halt briefly in a covered area designated by the platoon leader. This area is usually part of a company or battalion assembly area. Immediately on arrival in this area the squad leader disperses his men in the area allotted him by the platoon leader. He takes advantage of all natural cover and concealment to protect them from aerial and ground observation and fire. Every man must take advantage of existing holes or furrows, or must be required to dig an individual prone shelter, so that his body will be below the level of the ground in order to reduce the danger from bomb or shell fragments.

(2) The squad may furnish an interior guard for the platoon; the principal duty of such a guard is to see that men do not congregate or expose themselves or their equipment to hostile observation. It also may post one or more sentinels to guard against surprise attack by hostile patrols or may furnish air-antitank guards.

(3) As soon as his men are disposed in the assembly area, the squad leader inspects the physical condition and equipment of every man. Extra ammunition usually is issued in the assembly area. The squad leader insures that each man receives the proper quantities and types.

b. Reconnaissance.—The squad leader may move forward in advance of his squad to receive the platoon leader's attack order, or may receive it after the squad has left the assembly area and arrived in the vicinity from which the attack is to start. He may be able to reconnoiter or observe the ground over which his squad is to attack in much the same manner as described in paragraph par. 110b for the platoon leader. If there is so little time remaining after receiving the platoon order that he must lead his squad at once into its position, the squad leader, during his return to the squad, selects a route of advance. Thereafter, having issued certain parts of his order, he precedes his squad and continues his reconnaissance as he advances. He never exposes his squad in an area subject to enemy small-arms fire without prior reconnaissance.

c. Squad attack order.—(1) The squad leader issues his attack order to all men of his squad. Orders are well executed only when they are clear and definite and all 12 minds in the squad understand the squad mission and the plan for accomplishing that mission. To be certain that nothing is left out, a definite sequence is followed. The squad leader—

(*a*) Tells the men all that he knows about the enemy and about his own troops that they do not already know and which directly affect their conduct in the action.

(*b*) Tells the men what the squad is to do and what his plan is for doing it.

(*c*) Tells each man what he is to do. If all are to do the same thing, there is no need to tell each one separately.

(*d*) Tells the squad where he is going to be. When he is to be at a distance from the squad, he tells them exactly where he will be. For example: "I will be ahead of the squad, with the scouts, in those bushes" (pointing to them).

(*e*) Squad leaders can most effectively give instructions to their squads under cover. It is very difficult to communicate instructions and insure their execution after the squads have occupied the firing position.

Formation or patrol passing through village.

144. CONDUCT OF ATTACK.—*a. Movement to attack.*—The squad usually moves from the assembly area to the area from which it is to start its attack under control of the platoon leader or company commander. This movement is a continuation of the approach march. The platoon leader's attack order will direct that the squad start its attack on a prescribed signal or at a specified time. The squad may be directed to attack from a certain small area or from the vicinity of a certain point. The squad must be in its assigned place, ready to move forward or commence firing, at the prescribed time. Sometimes, however, the squad is directed to cross a certain road or other "line of departure" on a prescribed signal or at a specified time. In this situation, the squad should be held under cover a short distance in rear of the designated line until just before the time of attack. If possible, the start of its movement should be so timed that, without halting, its leading man crosses the line at the specified moment.

b. Fire and movement.—(1) Unless otherwise ordered by the platoon leader, the squad leader permits his squad to open fire only when fire action is necessary to cover a further advance. At the first firing position, the squad seeks to gain fire superiority over the enemy to its front. Fire superiority is gained by subjecting the enemy to fire of such accuracy and intensity that his fire becomes so inaccurate or so reduced in volume as to be ineffective; once gained, it must be maintained. Unless supporting weapons or other units are able to maintain fire superiority without any help from the squad, enough members of the squad must remain in position and continue the fire to maintain it. The automatic rifle's capacity for putting down a large volume of fire makes it especially useful for this purpose. Meanwhile, other members of the squad move forward, take up firing positions closer to the enemy, and, by their fire, cover the forward movement of the rearward members. By this combination of fire and movement, the squad advances close enough to capture the hostile position by assault.

(2) When the squad begins firing, the method of its further advance is determined by the effectiveness of the hostile fire and by the terrain features affording cover. The squad must take advantage of every irregularity of the ground to provide protection against hostile fire. Complete fire superiority is required for men to advance over open ground in the face of an unbeaten enemy. The squad can advance as a unit only when completely defiladed from hostile small-arms fire or when the hostile fire is kept neutralized by the fire of other units or of supporting weapons. Therefore, the squad usually works forward by irregular or successive advances of individuals.

(3) Rushes by individuals or small groups are used to move from cover to cover across short stretches of terrain. Even in very open terrain the well-trained rifleman will be able to locate and use all kinds of limited cover, such as slight depressions or rises. However, in very open areas, an advance will usually necessitate overwhelming fire superiority with consequent longer bounds between firing

positions. To leave a covered position, make a short rush, and drop into a position which affords no protection from enemy ground fire, serves only to increase losses without commensurate gain.

(4) The automatic rifleman supports the rapid advance of other members of the squad from flank positions. Because of the difficulty of maintaining an adequate supply of ammunition, the fire of automatic rifles is conserved to the actual needs of the situation. Thus, when the fires of individual riflemen serve to accomplish the desired effect, they are used in preference to the automatic rifle.

(5) The squad increases its rate of fire during periods when any part of it or of an adjacent squad is in movement.

(6) When the squad leader decides to advance with certain individuals, he turns command of the remaining men over to the assistant squad leader. The assistant squad leader causes the remaining men to advance on his orders. The squad leader decides whether the automatic rifleman will accompany him in the first group of individuals or remain under the control of the assistant squad leader. In other situations, the squad leader may direct that his assistant control the advance of the first few individuals, while the squad leader remains in his present position. Exceptionally, when the squad is able to advance in a single rush, the squad leader gives the necessary commands. The intensity of the hostile resistance and the available cover will indicate which method should be used.

(7) (*a*) In moving forward from one firing position to another, and if a defiladed area is available behind the new position, the men are halted in rear of it. The squad leader creeps forward quickly to locate and observe the target, and to decide where to place the individual members of his squad. First he selects a position for the automatic rifleman; then he decides how and where to employ his riflemen. He requires the men to move forward and observe the target with a minimum of exposure and gives his preliminary fire orders (sight setting and description of the target). He then commands "fire position," and his men crawl to a position from which they can open fire on the target at the leader's signal. The squad leader then orders or signals "commence firing."

(*b*) When this method cannot be followed, the squad leader may designate the new firing position to the first individuals to advance, send them forward, and thereafter build up the new firing line with other men as they arrive. At times it may be necessary to advance to a new firing position merely by signaling "forward" to individuals or groups in the squad and then leaving it up to the leading element to select the new firing position.

c. Position and duties of squad leader.—(1) During the fire fight, the primary duty of the squad leader is to place the fire of his squad on the target. He enforces fire discipline. The squad leader takes a position from which he can best control his men and observe the effect of their fire. In selecting his position, he considers the necessity of maintaining contact with the platoon leader. At times, on account of the noise and confusion of battle, the leader may have to go to the firing line and move from man to man to give instructions. He fires only in emergency, or when he considers that the fire power to be gained by his firing outweighs the necessity for his close control of his squad. Experienced soldiers may be designated to supervise the fire discipline of the two or three men in their immediate vicinity.

(2) When the squad leader cannot personally maintain effective control over the fire of the squad as a whole, he may retain control over a portion and temporarily delegate control over the remainder to the assistant squad leader.

(3) He requires that firing be limited to enemy troops or those positions (small areas) where enemy troops are known or believed to be located.

(4) He looks ahead for firing positions which his squad can use as the platoon moves forward.

(5) He seeks a position for his automatic rifleman which permits flanking fire to be delivered on any target across the entire squad front.

(6) He is constantly on the alert to advance his squad to a location nearer the enemy.

(7) He is responsible for maintaining contact with the platoon leader at all times; he may delegate this duty to the assistant squad leader.

(8) He prevents the members of his squad from becoming so widely separated that he loses control.

(9) He prevents several men from bunching behind cover suitable for only one man. Isolated trees, stumps, bushes, or other well-defined objects should be avoided.

(10) He observes the location of units on his flanks and makes a prompt report to the platoon leader whenever wide gaps occur in the attacking echelon.

(11) During lulls in the fight, the squad leader checks ammunition and has ammunition collected from the dead and wounded.

(12) In the absence of instructions from the platoon leader, particularly during the last stages of the fire fight, the squad leader may often have to attack important or dangerous targets without orders.

(13) He resists by fire sudden attacks from the flanks.

(14) If the squad becomes separated from its platoon, he makes every effort to locate and join the nearest friendly troops. The squad leader then takes orders from the leader of these troops. At the first favorable opportunity the squad is released and rejoins its platoon.

d. Position and duties of assistant squad leader.—The assistant squad leader's position is not fixed; he takes position where he can best assist the squad leader and be prepared to protect the squad from tank attack. He usually assists in enforcing fire discipline, controlling the fire, supervising the replenishment of ammunition, and maintaining contact with the platoon leader. He may be required to fire caliber .30 ammunition when the squad leader believes his fire is necessary. He is always prepared to fire antitank rifle grenades on hostile tanks coming within range.

145. ASSAULT.—The assault is delivered on orders, on signal of the platoon leader, or on the initiative of the squad leader. It is delivered at the earliest moment that promises success and without regard to the progress of adjacent squads. The squad approaches the hostile resistance by keeping as close as practicable to the supporting fires. When these fires are lifted, the squad may employ assault fire to prevent the enemy from manning his position. In the final stage of the assault the hostile position is overrun in a single rush with the bayonet. Against an intrenched enemy, the final charge may be preceded by a hand-grenade volley.

146. ASSAULT FIRE.—Assault fire is the fire delivered by a unit during its assault on a hostile position. Automatic riflemen and riflemen, with bayonets fixed, all taking full advantage of existing cover such as tanks, boulders, trees, walls, and mounds, advance rapidly toward the enemy and fire as they advance at areas known or believed to be occupied by hostile personnel. Such fire is usually delivered from the standing position and is executed at a rapid rate.

147. REORGANIZATION.—After a successful assault, the squad leader reorganizes his squad and prepares to advance or to repel hostile counterattacks.

148. SUPPORT SQUAD.—*a.* Before the attack, the squad leader of a squad in support informs his men of the situation and proposed action of the platoon. He advances his squad in accordance with the orders or signals of the platoon leader or platoon sergeant, keeping it under cover as far as practicable, and preventing it from merging with the attacking squads.

b. When directed to reinforce the attacking squads, he points out the positions of the enemy and of the attacking squads. He indicates the part of the line to be reinforced and prepares the squad for a rush, extending intervals if necessary.

c. If ordered to attack a definitely located hostile resistance from a flank, the squad leader locates a departure position for the attack and the best-covered route of approach thereto. He then moves the squad, preceded when necessary by scouts, to the position selected, and endeavors to overwhelm the enemy by opening surprise fire and delivering the assault from an unexpected direction.

SECTION III
DEFENSE

149. GENERAL.—The platoon leader's defense order assigns to the rifle squad the general trace of the line to be occupied, a specific sector of fire, and general locations and principal directions of fire for the automatic rifleman and the antitank rifle grenadier. The location of each member of the squad and the assignment of individual sectors of fire is a function of the squad leader. As soon as the squad reaches the position, the automatic rifle is set up and prepared to fire.

150. SQUAD DEFENSE ORDER.—Upon receipt of the platoon defense order the squad leader looks over his areas and notes the locations of adjacent squads and any supporting weapons for which he must provide close protection. He then issues his order to the squad. The order covers:

   a. The enemy situation.

   b. Location of adjacent squads and supporting weapons.

   c. The extent of the squad area and sector of fire.

   d. General location for each member of the squad.

   e. Location of command posts of the platoon and company.

151. ORGANIZATION OF THE SQUAD DEFENSE AREA.—*a.* The squad leader then has each man lie down in a firing position. Individuals are placed at least five yards apart. He then adjusts their positions until each man is able to cover the desired sector of fire. Minor clearing is accomplished in the immediate foreground and foxholes or slit trenches are constructed.

   b. The squad leader assigns a sector of fire to each firing member of his squad. Adjacent individual sectors of fire overlap. The field of fire of the weapon on the extreme flank of the squad includes the front of the adjacent squad.

   c. The automatic rifle is located where it can accomplish the mission assigned by the platoon leader. The sector of fire for the automatic rifle includes the squad sector of fire and the front of adjacent squads.

   d. After the squad digs in, the squad leader examines his position from the direction of the enemy to check on individual camouflage. Special emphasis is placed on concealing the position from both ground and air observation.

   e. To expedite the opening of fire, ranges are estimated to the most important landmarks in the squad sector of fire.

   f. The squad leader takes position where he can best observe the squad area and exercise control. He posts the assistant squad leader where he can cover with his antitank rifle grenades the most favorable approach for hostile tanks, and assist in exercising control.

g. As time and other duties permit, the squad leader prepares in duplicate a rough sketch of the squad's sector of fire showing prominent terrain features with the estimated ranges thereto. He submits the sketch to the platoon leader and retains a copy for his own use.

[...]

153. CONDUCT OF DEFENSE.—*a.* During a hostile preparatory bombardment the squad takes cover in its prepared positions. As soon as the artillery fire or aerial bombing lifts, firing positions are taken to meet the hostile attack. Fire is withheld until the enemy comes within effective rifle range (500 yards).

b. Members of the squad open fire upon an approaching enemy on command of the squad leader, given in accordance with the platoon leader's orders. The success of the defense depends upon each squad defending in place. If enemy riflemen enter the squad area, they are driven out by fire, grenades, and the bayonet. A stubborn defense in place by front-line squads breaks up enemy attack formations, and makes him vulnerable to counterattacks by higher units. *The squad withdraws only on orders of a higher commander.*

154. NIGHT WITHDRAWAL.—In a night withdrawal, the squad leader withdraws his men at the designated time direct to the rear and assembles them in the first position which affords cover. He then forms squad column and conducts the squad to the platoon assembly area.

155. DAYLIGHT WITHDRAWAL.—When the squad is ordered to withdraw during daylight, individuals are sent to the rear, thinning out the squad as rapidly as possible; those left in position cover this withdrawal. The squad leader withdraws with the last man of the squad, usually the automatic rifleman. The men retire from cover to cover, taking advantage of defiladed routes. The assistant squad leader, or a designated member of the squad, assembles the squad as rapidly as possible at the platoon assembly area.

SECTION IV
SECURITY MISSIONS

156. GENERAL.—The rifle squad may be detailed to provide security for a larger unit, to perform reconnaissance missions, or to defend obstacles. The rifle squad or fraction thereof, in performing security or reconnaissance missions, may be classified either as a security patrol or as a reconnaissance patrol.

157. SECURITY PATROLS.—*a. General.*—In order to perform their missions, security patrols usually are required to fight when they gain contact with hostile forces. Therefore the half-squad on a security patrol mission often includes the automatic rifleman. Security patrols regulate their movement with reference to the unit they are protecting. Such patrols are further classified as follows:

    (1) Point of advance, flank, or rear guard.

    (2) Flank security patrol.

    (3) Connecting group.

    (4) March outpost.

    (5) Outguards.

    b. Point of advance guard.—(1) The point is the name given the few infantrymen (usually a rifle squad or half-squad) sent forward by the advance party. Motorized reconnaissance and security elements from higher units usually precede the point.

    (2) The point of an advance guard moves along the axis of advance; it gives warning of the presence of any enemy that may have eluded motorized or mechanized covering forces; and prevents an enemy in the immediate vicinity of the route of march from opening surprise fire on the troops in rear.

    (3) The point precedes the advance party by a distance varying with the nature of the terrain, but usually, not exceeding 300 yards. To permit control by the squad leader, reduce the danger from hostile small-arms fire, and facilitate prompt fire action toward the front or either flank, the point marches in column of twos with one file on each side of the road and with a minimum of 5 paces between individuals. Two scouts precede the point by 50 to 100 yards. The squad leader may go wherever his presence is demanded, usually near the head of the point. The assistant squad leader marches at the tail of the point.

    (4) The point fires on all hostile elements within effective rifle range. The presence of a distant enemy, beyond effective rifle range, is reported by the signal, "enemy in sight"; the point continues to advance until within effective range; it then opens fire and endeavors to drive the enemy off. When forced by enemy fire to stop, or when unable to drive off the enemy, the point holds its position and covers the action of the advance party. Rapid, aggressive movement and fire action by the point not only may drive off small enemy groups, but may force a large enemy group to commit itself to fire action and disclose its dispositions; and thus materially assist the rapid and effective employment of the advance party.

    (5) The point observes toward the front and flanks, but executes no flank reconnaissance.

(6) Except to open fire, the point stops only when so ordered by the advance party commander. When the column halts, the point sends forward one or more observers to guard against surprise attack.

c. Point of flank guard.—The point of a flank guard performs its missions in accordance with the instructions of the platoon leader, and in a manner similar to that prescribed for the point of an advance guard.

d. Point of rear guard.—(1) The rear point is the name given to the few infantrymen (usually a rifle squad or half-squad) farthest to the rear in a column on the march. It is detailed from the rear party.

(2) The dispositions of a rear point are similar to those of a point of an advance guard, in reverse order.

(3) The rear point stops to fire only when enemy action threatens to interfere with the march. It signals the rear party commander when the enemy is observed.

(4) The rear point can expect no reinforcement from other troops. When the enemy presses closely, other troops take up a position farther to the rear; the rear point, when forced back, withdraws around a flank or designated route so as not to mask their fire.

e. Connecting files.—(1) Connecting files are furnished by the larger units to keep contact with the next smaller unit in the direction of the enemy.

(2) Connecting files pass forward all orders and messages received from the unit sending them out. They halt only on orders or signals from that unit, or when the smaller unit halts. They pass back to the larger unit no signals except "enemy in sight," and special signals previously agreed upon.

(3) If a connecting file consists of one man, he looks alternately to the rear and to the front for signals. When the connecting file consists of two men (double connecting file), one man looks to the rear for signals, the other to the front; and they remain near enough to each other to communicate by voice.

f. Flank security patrol.—General.—(*a*) Throughout the various phases of an attack, as well as in defense, a rifle squad or half-squad may be sent out as a flank security patrol. Such a patrol may be told to go to a certain place, or simply to move generally abreast of the attacking echelon.

(*b*) If the patrol is to remain for a time at one locality, the leader selects, and has prepared, one or more firing positions for each man, to insure all-around defense. The half-squad posts one man to observe; the squad usually posts two men; another man watches for signals from the unit whose flank is being protected. The remainder of the patrol remains under cover, ready to go immediately to the selected firing positions.

(*c*) If the patrol is not directed to a specific location, the leader must choose a position from which he can protect the flank of his unit by holding off the enemy, or at least by giving warning of his approach.

(*d*) In the absence of instructions, the patrol leader moves his patrol so as to protect the flank of the unit sending him out. He selects routes and successive positions which enable him to perform his mission and at the same time to maintain contact with the unit protected. He details one or more men to observe constantly for signals, and informs his commander of his movements and plans, by messengers or visual signals.

(2) *On the march.*—(*a*) A rifle squad or half-squad is often detailed to act as a flank security patrol for a unit on the march. The squad leader is given orders either to go to a designated locality, remain for a specified time and then rejoin the column, or to march along a certain route or at a specified distance to the flank. Flank patrols may be required to move an equal distance in a shorter time than the main body, or a longer distance in the same time. Therefore, when vehicles are available, it may be highly desirable to provide them with motor transportation.

(*b*) The patrol moves so as to prevent the enemy from placing small-arms fire on the column within midrange (400–600 yards). It investigates areas likely to conceal hostile elements and locations which might permit good observation by the enemy on and near the route of the patrol. It observes from commanding ground and moves rapidly from point to point so as to keep between the protected unit and possible locations of hostile elements.

(*c*) Hostile elements are reported by signal or messenger; large forces advancing toward the main body are reported both by signal and messenger. Hostile patrols moving away from the main body are reported but are not fired on; all other hostile forces within effective range are immediately attacked by fire. If the enemy opens fire either on the patrol or on the column, the patrol determines his strength and dispositions, and reports these promptly to the column commander. Meanwhile, the patrol resists to the last man an enemy attack on the column, unless ordered to withdraw.

(*d*) Contact with the patrol is maintained by the commander of the unit sending it out.

g. Connecting group.—(1) A rifle squad, half-squad, or smaller fraction sent to the flank of a company or platoon to keep in contact with the unit on that flank is called a connecting group. It moves and operates so that it knows at all times the location of the near flank of each unit with which it is keeping contact.

(2) If an adjacent unit falls behind, immediate report should be made to the commander who sent out the group. The connecting group may be divided into two

smaller patrols in order to cover the widened interval and maintain contact with both units.

(3) If contact with the adjacent unit is lost, a report of that fact is made immediately by messenger to the commander who sent out the group. Unless ordered to return, the group remains out to protect the flank and becomes a flank security patrol.

(4) While maintaining contact, the connecting group fires only for self-protection or to give warning of a flank attack by the enemy.

h. March outpost.—When detailed as a march outpost and assigned an area of observation, a squad leader places his squad under cover so as to maintain thorough observation of his area. Men are assigned to reliefs to insure alert observation.

i. Outguards.—(1) A squad, or a portion thereof, may be detailed as an outguard of an outpost for bivouac area. The support commander prescribes the posts of the outguard and the number of sentinels. Sentinels are designated as "Sentinel No.____, Outguard No.____, Support No.____."

(2) The outguard commander selects the posts for sentinels covering his sector of observation. During the day they are placed primarily to observe; at night, to listen. At night it may be necessary to change the positions of the sentinels. Any talking at night must be in whispers.

(3) Sentinels are given the following information:

(*a*) As to enemy:

    1. Direction.

    2. Patrol or other activity in the area.

    3. Special sector to watch.

(*b*) As to own troops:

    1. Location of the support and outguards to the right and left, and number of his relief.

    2. Any patrols which have gone out and will return through his post.

    3. Where prisoners are to be taken and where messages are to be sent.

(*c*) Special signals, such as gas alarm and countersigns.

(*d*) Names of features of military importance, such as roads, villages, or streams.

    1. Members of the outguard not posted as sentinels rest nearby under cover (natural cover if available, otherwise individual protective trenches) but remain fully equipped and close to their weapons.

2. The outguard commander is told what to do if the enemy attacks. When his orders direct that he resist a hostile attack, he causes individual firing emplacements to be dug.

158. RECONNAISSANCE PATROLS.—*a.* Reconnaissance patrols are used primarily to secure information, maintain contact with the enemy, or observe terrain. They usually consist of a leader and three to five men. They avoid unnecessary combat and accomplish their mission by stealth. They engage in fire fights only when necessary for the successful accomplishment of their mission or to protect themselves. They regulate their movements and locations with reference to their mission, and are not required to maintain contact with the unit which they serve. Automatic riflemen should *not* ordinarily be detailed with reconnaissance patrols, because such a mission requires mobility and stealth rather than fire power.

b. Orders to the patrol leader state the information of the enemy, mission, objective, general routes to be followed, the outpost or other security elements through which the patrol is to pass, time of return, and place where messages are to be sent or the patrol is to report. If the patrol is to return at a point different from its exit from the friendly lines, friendly troops at that point must be informed. Orders often are given to the entire patrol unless it is led by an officer.

c. Prior to departure, the patrol leader studies a map and the terrain, and selects a suitable route. He designates alternate leaders, informs the men of the situation, mission of the patrol, terrain to be crossed, individual tasks, special signals, and the assembly point in case the patrol is forced to separate. He prescribes what items of clothing are to be left behind and insures that each man carries a full canteen of water and the necessary rations. He inspects the patrol to insure that arms and equipment will not glisten or rattle, and that no letters or documents are carried. On leaving the friendly lines, the patrol leader informs the nearest outguard or front-line unit of his proposed route and obtains available information concerning the enemy and friendly patrols operating in the vicinity.

d. A reconnaissance patrol usually advances by bounds from one covered position to another. Bounds are short near the enemy. When approaching a dangerous area, the patrol leader sends a scout ahead, while the others cover his advance. The scout signals "forward" if all is clear and remains in observation while the rest of the patrol advances.

e. (1) In searching woods, the patrol moves in a thin skirmish line. The interior of the woods is carefully reconnoitered by successive advances to clearings or trail junctions.

(2) A patrol usually moves along the heights on one or both sides of ravine or cut. If necessary to pass through a defile, the patrol adopts a staggered formation

Method of approaching house and crossing stream.

and keeps close to the sides. If the distance to be traversed is short, a scout is sent to the far side to observe; the remainder of the patrol does not enter the defile until he signals "forward." If the distance is too great or observation is limited, a scout moves by bounds at least 150 yards ahead of the patrol.

(3) Before a stream is crossed, the opposite bank is carefully observed. A scout crosses first; the other members of the patrol cover his advance and cross after he has made a brief reconnaissance.

(4) On approaching a cross road, a patrol halts and sends scouts to the flanks to reconnoiter the side roads. The patrol advances when all is reported clear.

f. (1) By day, patrols are usually controlled by arm-and-hand signals and oral orders. By night, they are controlled by voice and by prearranged sound signals.

(2) Success in night patrolling depends largely upon the ability to move silently and maintain direction and control. Before starting, the patrol leader determines the compass direction and location of prominent objects near his route. In planning the route, he endeavors to avoid terrain features which hinder movement. Dispositions are similar to those adopted during daylight, but distances and intervals are reduced.

g. Prearranged signals, audible for only a short distance, such as rustling of paper, snapping the edge of a matchbox with the finger nail, or tapping the helmet, are used to control the patrol. Oral orders and whispering are limited to emergencies. Signals to stop the patrol and move it forward are often given by the leading scout but may be given by any member in an emergency. Whoever halts the patrol is responsible for starting it again. A check-up signal, given by the patrol leader to verify the presence of all men, is answered according to a prearranged plan.

h. If a patrol is attacked, the man who first notes the danger calls out, "front," "right," "left," or "rear." All members face toward the man attacked. The men on the flanks advance a short distance straight ahead and then close on the enemy from the flanks. The patrol leader and any men with him rush the enemy. During the combat, the members of the patrol repeat their recognition signals. The patrol leader designates a get-away man to stay out of the fight so that he can return with the information obtained in case the other members of the patrol are killed or captured.

i. The patrol leader decides whether information gained is to be sent back at once by messenger or reported on the return of the patrol. An example of a message which a patrol leader might send back is shown on the next page. After the message is written, the patrol leader points out to the messenger the location of the stone fence, woods, and machine guns. He then is told what the patrol leader intends to do. This sketch can be made quickly and requires no special ability. It contains all necessary information. If the commanding officer of Company A wants to know what the patrol leader intends doing, the messenger can supply the information. Thus, if the messenger and the message are captured by an enemy patrol there is nothing in the message to indicate where the patrol is now located. To have written "squad will remain at B" invites capture.

j. Since many night patrols are sent out to capture prisoners and execute tasks which may require combat, each patrol rehearses plans for night combat and laying ambushes until it is highly proficient. Only through repeated rehearsals and training can each member of the patrol learn to do his part unhesitatingly and correctly, and thus gain confidence in the ability of the patrol as a unit. Failure to do this results in heavy losses.

Example of a message from a patrol leader.

159. DEFENSE OF OBSTACLES.—*a.* A rifle squad, reinforced, frequently is detailed to cover an obstacle with fire. The members of the squad are so placed that they can sweep the outer edges of the obstacle by flanking fire.

b. When the squad is protecting a mine field, the squad leader establishes a warning patrol over the mine field area to prevent damage to friendly vehicles.

c. The men protecting the obstacle are concealed from hostile observation, and are placed at such distance from the obstacle as to be outside the zone of dispersion of artillery fire or dive bombing directed at the obstacle (200 to 400 yards).

The following extracts from *Organization and Tactics of Infantry: The Rifle Battalion* (1940) give due consideration to three of the most significant challenges for any U.S. infantry formation in World War II—attacks through woodland, assaults across river defense lines, and combat in villages. The horrors of woodland fighting have already been outlined in the introduction, when we reflected upon the fighting in the Hürtgen forest in 1944, but the U.S. experienced arboreal combat in many other locations besides. In such circumstances, an aerial breakwater of trees prevented the effective use of artillery and air power, while at ground level the tree-trunks, foliage, and folds in the ground provided both the defenders and the attackers with ample cover and concealment, but little long-range visibility, creating the perfect recipe for close-quarters combat.

River defenses were another frequent challenge faced by the Allied troops, both in Italy and norther Europe. In January 1944, for example, the 141st and 143rd Infantry Regiments of the U.S. 36th Infantry Division made the first of several attempts at a combat crossing of the Gari River, south of Monte Cassino. The small-boat crossings were conducted in the face of the most horrifying German firepower, destroying many craft and killing or wounding hundreds of men on the open water. Those who did make it across were trapped and either destroyed or captured. Final U.S. casualties were 1,330 dead and wounded and 770 captured.

Village combat was a frequent punctuation of the advance across Europe. The Germans were masters of turning even the humblest collection of buildings into formidable defenses, especially by setting up machine guns in positions where U.S. infantry units would be caught in lethal crossfire. Only systematic and disciplined approaches to small-unit movement, plus the application of crushing firepower, could win through.

From FM 7-5, *Organization and Tactics of Infantry:*
The Rifle Battalion **(1940)**

CHAPTER 4
SPECIAL PHASES OF OPERATIONS

SECTION I
COMBAT IN WOODS

132. CHARACTERISTICS.—Combat in wooded areas results in decreased effectiveness of all fire and of mechanized forces; increases the importance of close combat and surprise; impedes the maintenance of direction, control, and communication; promotes concealment and effectiveness of ambushes; and increases chemical effect. Special training in this type of combat is necessary.

133. ATTACK.—*a. General*—The attack of a woods comprises the advance over open ground to the edge of the woods, the advance through the woods, and the egress therefrom. The forward and rear edges, crossroads, and important lateral routes of communications within the woods usually are intermediate objectives.

b. Attack of forward edge.—The forward edge is taken by methods similar to those used against any terrain objective. The defender observes the advancing troops from his own concealed position. Smoke may be used to neutralize this advantage; or the approach to the edge of the woods may be made at night. The advance continues after reorganization just within the woods.

c. Advance within woods.—(1) The advance within the woods is organized to maintain cohesion between attacking units. Precautions are used to prevent loss of direction. Compass directions are always assigned. Movement is by bounds with periodic halts to restore contact and cohesion, either on predetermined lines or at prescribed periods. Paths or roads perpendicular to the direction of advance are especially useful lines upon which to coordinate the advance of the heads of the leading elements and gain control.

(2) Dispositions depend on the difficulty of movement and the visibility within the wood. In sparse woods the leading elements are in line of skirmishers. In dense woods the advance is in line of small columns. Scouts precede and reconnoiter to the front and flanks, remaining preferably within sight of their units. As soon as the scouts have indicated that all is clear, the troops advance and the scouts move forward. When the scouts report an obstacle across the line of advance, additional reconnaissance is desirable to discover hostile posts located to sweep the obstacle with fire. Silence is maintained during the advance.

(3) The advance is a series of maneuvers to gain local objectives such as trail crossings and clearings. Upon encountering resistance, leading units usually seek to

Correct use of cover.

envelop its flanks, while units in rear and supporting weapons prepare to support the action. Against scattered resistance, an enveloping maneuver is launched as soon as practicable, with little support by artillery and infantry supporting weapons.

(4) Strong columns, echeloned in depth, are usually employed to advance along the lateral edges of a wood. They operate against the flanks of resistances holding up the attacking units in the wood.

d. Debouchment from a wood.—The troops debouch by surprise from the far side of a wood after reconnaissance and under the protection of a strong base of fire. Before debouchment, units halt and re-form far enough within the wood to be out of hostile view. The next position to be occupied is observed. If heavy fire from artillery on the edge of the wood may be expected as the units begin to debouch, the movement of the leading platoons may be carried out in a single rush. When danger is greater from close combat weapons than from artillery fire, the egress may be by infiltration. The next objective should mask the edge of the woods from hostile observation and screen the egress of subsequent echelons.

e. Small woods.—Small woods are usually neutralized by fire, outflanked, and later mopped up by reserve units.

134. DEFENSE.—*a. Value.*—(1) Isolated small woods usually attract artillery fire; however, they provide some protection against tanks. Decision to occupy them depends on the probable hostile artillery effect or likelihood of attack by hostile mechanized elements.

(2) Large wooded areas favor the construction of strong, well-concealed defense areas, surrounded by artificial obstacles. Such wooded areas impede offensive operations and enable weak forces to make a stubborn resistance.

(3) Large woods in rear of a position are of value for concealing reserves and communications and in covering withdrawals.

b. Location of main line of resistance.—(1) A wooded area may be defended by locating the main line of resistance in front of the woods, along the forward edge, within the woods, or in rear thereof. Tactical or terrain considerations are the determining factors.

(2) Usually the main line of resistance will be within the woods, with the forward edge of the woods held by *security* detachments. If the main line of resistance within the wood is oblique to the outpost position located outside the woods, it affords flanking fires and deceives the enemy.

c. Fire plan.—(1) The defense of the main line of resistance within a wood is organized to surprise the attack with a dense system of close-in defensive fires. Roads, paths, and trails are enfiladed by rifle and machine-gun fires. Cleared spaces and the forward edges of concealed obstacles are swept with flanking fires.

(2) Lanes are cut for machine-gun fires along the front and flanks of organized areas. Thinning trees and undergrowth is better than a complete clearing. The lack of observation for the control of fires frequently limits effectiveness of artillery and of infantry mortars. Where there are no naturally cleared areas available as battery positions, they are prepared. The flat trajectory of the field artillery guns requires more clearing than do the high-trajectory infantry mortars. Because of their greater range and defensive echelonment in depth, the gun batteries are usually able to find suitable natural cleared firing positions further in rear of the battle position. Artillery usually covers the intersections of roads and trails, defiles through which the hostile attacking Infantry will have to pass, and likely hostile assembly areas. The high-angle fire of infantry mortars permits the 81-mm platoon to be sited in limited cleared areas, and its plunging fire is affected but little by the trees as the projectiles strike. The 60-mm mortars are usually attached to rifle platoons, where their fire can be directed by the platoon leader against enemy attacking dispositions as they are disclosed during the attack.

(3) Concealment of a few riflemen in trees often adds to the effectiveness of the defense.

d. Organization of defense.—(1) The lateral edges are strongly defended in order to prevent outflanking action.

(2) A small holding garrison may be located in rear of a shallow wood to enfilade enveloping attacks, to support counterattacks, and prevent the enemy from debouching in case he penetrates the wood.

(3) Obstacles are erected to protect the main line of resistance, prevent the use of paths and trails, canalize the hostile advance into areas swept by the fire of concealed automatic weapons, and cause the attack to lose direction and impetus. Routes are reconnoitered and marked.

e. Distribution of troops.—(1) Limited fields of view and fire require reduction of distances and intervals between groups and individuals with consequent initial diminution of the depth and frontages of units. The strength of effectives required to hold a wood may be reduced after it has been properly organized.

(2) Areas held by front-line platoons are elongated and usually approach a linear formation. Local reserves, prepared for immediate counterattack, are disposed in smaller and more numerous groups than in open terrain.

(3) So far as practicable, the defense avoids the occupation of points easily identified on maps or which can be accurately located by hostile ground or air observation.

(4) When the defensive position is within the wood or in rear thereof, the forward edge is usually occupied by small detachments to observe and delay the enemy and screen the main line of resistance.

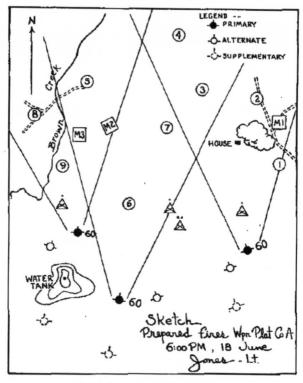

Sketch showing prepared mortar fires.

f. Chemicals.—Chemicals are highly effective in woods. Areas which have been subjected to concentrations of highly persistent gas should be evacuated.

SECTION II
NIGHT OPERATIONS

135. OBJECT.—The object of night operations may be to concentrate secretly before an attack; to approach a hostile position for an attack at daybreak; to cross a zone made impassable by hostile fire by day; to withdraw; to attack; to reconnoiter; to make a relief; to execute works; or to bring up supplies.

136. CHARACTERISTICS.—*a. Decrease in effectiveness of aimed fire.*—With poor observation, the effectiveness of aimed fire is greatly decreased. The importance of

the defensive fire of fixed weapons that can be laid on a definite line of fire by day is increased correspondingly.

b. Difficulty of movement.—Maintenance of direction, control, contact, and communication between units is extremely difficult. However, decrease in the effectiveness of fire permits denser formations.

c. Sensitive morale.—Troops at night are impressionable. The importance of surprise by the offense and of the preparation of ambushes by the defense is consequently increased.

137. MARCHES.—Night marches must be carefully prepared. Whenever practicable, the route is reconnoitered and marked prior to the commencement of the march. Columns are kept well closed up, distances are greatly reduced, guides are stationed at cross roads to prevent the wrong routes being taken, and numerous connecting files are provided. Special attention is given to the avoidance of lights and noise. Daybreak should find the troops in position or in concealed localities. When it is important to avoid observation by hostile airplanes, the command, so far as practicable, should march in small units and avoid main routes.

138. CROSS-COUNTRY MOVEMENTS.—*a.* In movements off roads at night, the route should be plotted and the march directed by the compass. A circuitous route which follows easily distinguishable terrain features is better than one more direct but less clearly marked.

b. An advance to terminate in an assault at daybreak should be so timed that the troops will arrive just before the assault is to be made.

139. ATTACK.—*a. General*—Although night attacks are difficult and hazardous operations, they are very effective when properly executed. Against an inferior or a demoralized enemy they are particularly effective.

b. Preliminary considerations.—(1) Troops for a night attack should be well trained and disciplined, in good physical condition, fresh, and under complete control initially.

(2) Open terrain favors control and movement and should be selected for the attack. Woods or badly cut-up ground render difficult the maintenance of direction, control, and contact. A well-defined line of departure near the objective and directly opposite it is desirable. The objective should be recognizable in the dark. Usually only short advances are practicable.

(3) Some visibility is desirable. A wind blowing from the direction of the defender promotes secrecy of the attack.

(4) The time of the attack depends upon the object sought. If the operation is a prelude to a daylight attack to exploit the success gained by the night attack, it

is launched shortly before daylight. The hour depends upon the time considered necessary to capture the objective and to reorganize. If capture and consolidation of the objective are not to be followed shortly by a further advance, the attack should be launched before midnight so that defense may be organized by daylight.

c. Orders.—(1) The attack order goes into greater detail than a similar order for an attack by day. Provision is made for every eventuality that reasonably can be foreseen.

(2) The order specifies routes of approach, assembly positions, line of departure, formations, compass direction of the attack, objective, means of identification of friendly troops, means of preserving secrecy and maintaining contact, action of the artillery and other supporting weapons, action to be taken upon capture of the objective, rallying points if checked, location of the reserve and its action, prearranged signals and communications, and when practicable the designation of the locality where secondary deployments will be made.

d. Preparation by subordinate units—(l) Commanders of units receiving orders for a night attack promptly warn their subordinate commanders so that they may make such daylight preparations as are not prohibited in the interests of secrecy.

(2) Daylight reconnaissance is essential. The line of departure is selected and marked, when practicable. Routes of advance are located and identified. Compass bearings are taken, and direction points which can be identified at night are chosen. Features such as streams, fences, ravines, ridges, roads, or telegraph lines running in the desired direction are noted, and the route of advance definitely selected. Plans are made to avoid or remove any obstacles that might impede or confuse the advancing troops.

(3) Troops are given as much rest as practicable before the attack. Hot food shortly before the attack is desirable.

e. Cooperation of other arms—(l) Artillery fires supporting a night attack must be prearranged. Requests for such fires must be made as early as possible to permit their preparation. Artillery fires or preparations should avoid arousing the enemy's suspicions prior to the attack. Artillery should be ready to place heavy fire on the hostile position to cover withdrawal of the attacking Infantry, should the assault be repulsed.

(2) Aviation may drop flares behind the hostile lines to guide attacking troops, and when the attack succeeds, may illuminate the terrain over which hostile counterattacks might be launched.

(3) Engineers demolish obstacles and help organize captured ground.

(4) Chemical warfare units may interdict likely avenues of approach after the position has been captured, or screen the position at daylight.

f. Maneuver.—Only the simplest maneuvers are likely to succeed in a night attack. Units must attack straight to the front. Detours of a few yards are permissible for individuals or small parties.

g. Advance.—(1) The advance is made in compact columns until close to the enemy. Partial deployment into squad columns with reduced intervals and distances is made by the leading elements at selected points before coming within assaulting distance. Bayonets are fixed before contact with the enemy is expected, and far enough away so that he cannot hear the sound. Rifles are unloaded.

(2) The leading unit of each column acts as a covering detachment. An officer moves ahead, preceded at the limit of visibility by scouts. The officer is followed closely by a selected group, including men speaking the hostile language. The advance is made by short bounds; at each halt the scouts reconnoiter for the next advance. Halts are of the shortest possible duration. If a hostile sentinel challenges, answer is made in the enemy's language, and the scouts and the group at the head of the column close in with the bayonet without firing; the rest of the troops lie down. Similar action is taken if the enemy fires one or two shots; precautions must be taken to prevent desultory firing by the enemy from bringing on a premature assault.

(3) Officers with compasses constantly check the direction of advance. An officer or noncommissioned officer marches at the rear of each column to prevent straggling and enforce silence.

(4) A silent, stealthy advance is necessary for surprise. Talking and rifle fire are prohibited. Units which lose contact with adjacent units continue to press forward toward their own objectives.

(5) The rate of advance varies with the terrain. Far from the enemy and over favorable terrain it may be a mile an hour. When closer to the enemy, the care necessary for secrecy should limit the rate of advance to 100 yards in from 6 to 10 minutes.

h. Assault.—The assault is delivered with the bayonet, without firing, when the attacking force is near enough to the hostile position or the enemy opens fire at close range. Hostile firing should not induce the troops to launch an assault from too great a distance. Aggressive leadership by officers and noncommissioned officers is required.

i. Reorganization.—Reorganization begins as soon as the objective is captured. Confusion and intermingling of units are corrected. Officers and noncommissioned officers form groups of men and place them in the more decisive localities. Losses are replaced or units combined as necessary.

140. DEFENSE.—*a.* The principal means of defense against night attack are the fires of fixed weapons, obstacles, illumination of the foreground, patrols and outguards, and counterassault.

b. These defensive means are combined to take the attacking forces by surprise. Ambushes are prepared by constructing concealed obstacles along the most probable routes of hostile advance and siting fixed weapons to sweep them with fire. Outguards provide for the security of the command, preparing ambushes in advanced positions to break the attack before it reaches the defensive position or to enable capture of hostile patrols. Local reserves are posted to recapture portions of the position which may be taken. Larger reserves must be able to form rapidly at designated assembly positions and proceed therefrom along previously reconnoitered routes to any part of the front where they may have to intervene. Large-scale counterattacks are usually postponed until daylight.

SECTION III
ATTACK AND DEFENSE OF RIVER LINES

141. MILITARY IMPORTANCE.—River lines are important military obstacles. Their protection against mechanized vehicles frequently determines the location of defensive or delaying positions. The military importance of a river line depends upon the width, depth of water, current, stream bed, banks, and facilities available for crossing.

142. HASTY CROSSING.—*a.* In an exploitation or a pursuit, attacking forces may come upon a stream line before the defender has time to utilize it as a barrier. Advance guards and pursuing detachments frequently have occasion to cross a river by surprise, making use of the means at hand, and under direction of the subordinate commanders on the ground. Such crossings are frequently made without the assistance of engineers or special equipment. Infantry commanders of leading units cross small detachments at selected points to seize a bridgehead on the enemy bank.

b. Crossing is accomplished by use of improvised means— boats found in the neighborhood, imperfectly destroyed bridges, etc. Where no means are immediately available, Infantry crosses by swimming and rafts made from its own equipment. All the combat equipment of a rifle company can be crossed with swimmers as follows:

(1) The 2-man rifle float can be prepared by 2 men in 7 minutes. The two shelter halves (one on top of the other) are placed on the ground, and the remainder of the two packs and the clothing of two soldiers are placed in the center of the canvas. The rifles (crossed to give rigidity) are placed on top of the packs and clothing. The float is completed by binding the four corners of the outside shelter half to the four extremities of the rifles by means of the shelter tent ropes. In a similar manner, using two 3-foot sticks or two shelter tent poles instead of rifles, a light machine gun, a 60-mm mortar, or two automatic rifles can be floated in a shelter tent.

(2) Ammunition and other supplies vital to the initial stage of the operation on the enemy side are apportioned to the two-men teams and ferried across.

c. In hasty crossing, control is left initially to the subordinate infantry commanders on whose initiative the crossing was effected. Higher commanders release additional means to their control until sufficient troops are across and the situation clarified by the successive commanders in the chain of command.

(1) Rapid exploitation of the hasty crossing by the small infantry units is necessary to prevent the enemy from concentrating against the isolated leading elements and destroying them. Detachments which have gained a footing on the far bank are reinforced at once; company commanders push forward to seize a bridgehead to cover a crossing point for additional troops.

(2) Higher commanders organize the crossing in force behind the most successful leading elements. Combat aviation is called upon to attack enemy forces concentrating against the bridgehead troops. Leading companies hold their positions regardless of losses until reinforcements from the battalion can reach their positions.

(3) Battalion commanders push heavy weapons forward promptly to reinforce the bridgehead elements. Fire support from the friendly bank is rarely practicable due to lack of observation and of liaison with the troops on the hostile bank.

(4) Control is usually by rifle company commanders, until sufficient forces have been crossed to build up a battalion defense area on the bridgehead positions. Regimental and higher commanders send antitank guns forward to points where they can be crossed quickly to protect the bridgehead troops from mechanized attack as their advance takes them into terrain where conditions for enemy mechanized attack are favorable.

(5) As the leading battalions establish themselves, lateral action to join initial battalion defense areas may be necessary to enlarge the bridgehead and protect construction of bridges for crossing the main body.

143. FORCED CROSSING.—*a.* A forced crossing is one made against alert enemy opposition. Such crossings are usually made at night, preferably shortly before daybreak. Every effort is made to insure surprise at the point of crossing. Fog and smoke may be used advantageously to screen a crossing at daybreak.

b. The initial crossing force (bridgehead troops) is assigned the mission of seizing a bridgehead for the crossing of the main body. The bridgehead is established at sufficient distance from the river to protect bridging operations from hostile ground observation and the remainder of the command from undue interruptions from hostile artillery fire.

(1) The first troops usually cross by assault boats or on foot bridges. The plan of crossing requires the leading infantry units to gain a foothold on the hostile bank by surprise; fire support by combat aviation or artillery is employed only after the enemy has discovered the crossing.

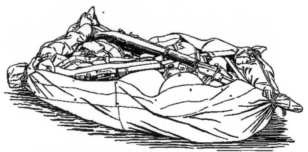

① **Rifle squad equipment prepared for river crossing.**

② **Rifle squad equipment floating.**

(2) If the enemy has organized the opposite bank and holds it in force, an aviation or artillery preparation may be employed to dislodge him and to protect engineering operations and the crossing of the Infantry. When the width of the river permits, an infantry base of fire may be established on the friendly bank to support the crossing of the leading companies; it deals chiefly with hostile automatic weapons covering the crossing points.

(3) Engineers may be attached to infantry battalions and at times to companies to assist in crossing streams. If the stream is wide, deep, or swift, the embarkation and crossing of the Infantry are usually under the direction of the engineers.

(4) The leading battalions select as initial objectives the points on their front from which the enemy can place observed small-arms fire on the crossing. These objectives are allotted to the leading companies and serve as assembly areas for continuation of the attack on the bridgehead objective. The company objectives should be easily recognizable by clearly defined features, such as a road, railroad, houses, etc., and usually include the slopes immediately dominating the stream.

(5) The leading battalions cross on a broad front. Rifle platoons cross simultaneously, land, and push forward to their company objectives.

(6) Platoon leaders select prominent features of the terrain to rally the boatloads of their men as they land. The river bank is cleared promptly. When rifle troops land in darkness they hold their fire, allow the enemy groups near the bank to disclose themselves by firing, then close with the bayonet.

(7) Rifle company commanders play no part in any melee which develops along the banks. They usually move with a composite group of their weapons platoon and a few selected bayonet fighters as protection. The group moves directly to the company objective, emplacing company weapons to repel a counterattack or to serve as a base of fire for further advance toward the bridgehead objective. The battalion commander sends his heavy weapons forward to reinforce his leading companies, personally crossing as soon as any of his leading companies have seized their objectives. He organizes the attack from assembly areas on the initial objective, employing such elements of the rifle companies as are available to form the spear head of the attack toward the next objective. The regimental commander attaches regimental weapons to leading battalions which have been successful and utilizes his reserve to extend the attack and secure the bridgehead position.

144. COORDINATION OF INFANTRY AND ENGINEERS.—*a. General.*— (1) A river crossing is an operation requiring close coordination of the leading infantry units and engineer troops charged with the supervision of the crossing.

(2) Success requires careful planning and a thorough understanding of the detailed arrangements by the subordinate infantry officers who must lead troops in the initial waves and the subordinate engineer officers who must put the boats in the water.

b. Reconnaissance.—(1) A ground, air, and map reconnaissance of the area is made by the commander or his representative and the engineer officer in charge to determine the points of crossing. Having decided upon the exact points of crossing, the engineer officer in charge makes a detailed reconnaissance to make measurements and to prepare technical plans for the crossing,

(2) Both tactical and technical considerations should be considered in the selection of the site, but tactical considerations are the governing factors.

(3) When time and concealment permit, reconnaissance should be made by commanders to include company commanders of the leading rifle companies.

(4) Reconnaissance activities are controlled so as not to disclose the plan to the enemy. Reconnaissance parties avoid detection from the air or the enemy side of the river.

c. Crossing of reserves.—Reserves of infantry regiments frequently cross in ponton boats or ferries, which have greater capacity than the assault boats used by leading battalions. They avoid all congestion or halts near the river bank. They may use their machine guns to reinforce the antiaircraft defense of the ferry site while they are crossing.

d. Antiaircraft security.—Air advantage is essential in river crossing. Antiaircraft weapons usually remain silent until the crossing is discovered by the enemy. Thereafter the neutralization of all hostile air operations over the crossing area is vital. The plan of antiaircraft defense includes the protection of the engineer bridging detachments in assembly areas, and during the advance to the river and the construction and operation of the bridges; and protection of the infantry covering troops in assembly areas, in ferrying operations, and in the construction and operation of the footbridges. Weapons of infantry supporting and reserve units may assist antiaircraft units, or be employed in lieu thereof, il antiaircraft fire missions.

e. Antitank security.—Bridgehead troops must be prepared for counterattacks, particularly by tanks, soon after their crossing. It is of utmost importance that antitank weapons be sent across with the leading companies so that they can reach the initial objective of these troops soon after the leading rifle platoons. Regimental antitank weapons (37-mm guns) are attached to the bridgehead battalions.

145. ASSEMBLY AREAS.—*a. Initial.*—Infantry battalions are moved to initial assembly areas for the crossing as close to the river line as is consistent with the general tactical plan. To avoid discovery by the enemy of the crossing front, initial battalion assembly areas are usually located within easy night marching distance of the river line.

b. Final.—(l) Final assembly areas are selected for each battalion crossing in the leading echelon. Frequently final assembly areas are assigned to each leading rifle company, the companies of each battalion marching directly from the battalion initial assembly area to company final assembly areas.

(2) The final assembly area is the point where assault boats are placed in readiness for the final carry by hand to the launching area at the river bank. Here the engineer crews are assigned to individual boats and await the arrival of the infantry troops of the bridgehead force in their movement forward from initial assembly areas.

(3) The assault boats are brought to the final assembly areas by truck when the terrain, the road net, and the requirements of secrecy permit. Engineer troops unload the boats and distribute them along the foot routes to the river so that they can be readily picked up by the carrying parties. Each boat is carried by the infantrymen who will cross in that boat.

(4) The principal requisites of the final assembly areas are—

(*a*) Accessibility to the trucks (or carrying parties) bringing up the assault boats.

(*b*) Concealment from hostile ground and aerial observation.

(*c*) Connection with, or proximity to, numerous easily followed foot routes to the river.

(*d*) Proximity to the actual crossing fronts.

(*e*) Distribution parallel to the front to allow both for crossing the river along the entire front and for proceeding directly and without delay to the embarkation points.

(*f*) Defilade or other protection from enemy rifle and artillery fire to be anticipated, even though secrecy may be preserved.

c. Engineer boat crews.—Two engineer soldiers are habitually assigned to each assault boat as crew; they guide and supervise the final approach to the river, the launching and loading of the boats, and all movement on the water.

146. MOVEMENT TO FINAL ASSEMBLY AREAS.—*a. Plans and orders.*— Plans for the movement are made to insure as little delay as practicable in final assembly areas and no delay at the river bank. Detailed orders for the crossing are issued in the initial assembly areas for each infantry unit crossing in the first wave. Orders for the movement to the river cover the following points:

(1) Location of the final assembly position for each company, routes thereto, and hour of arrival of each infantry unit at its own final assembly area.

(2) Method of control of march to final assembly areas (guides, control points, etc.)

(3) Number of boats assigned to each unit and capacity of each.

(4) Where contact is to be made with the engineer in charge of boats for each infantry rifle company (either at the initial or final assembly area).

b. Movement.—(1) The movement to the final assembly area is made under control of infantry leaders. Upon arrival at the final assembly area, engineer guides meet the infantry and conduct them to the boats. Subsequent movement to the river is under control of the engineer troops.

(2) Prior to leaving the initial assembly area, infantry units are divided into boat assignments. Tactical unity is maintained and adapted to the capacity of the boats.

(3) March dispositions are adopted which permit the troops to pick up their boats without change of formation. Orders or directions other than identification of units should not be necessary upon arrival at the final assembly area. The engineer guides lead units to the boats, the boats are picked up, and the unit moves on in silence.

147. MOVEMENT FROM FINAL ASSEMBLY AREA TO RIVER.—*a.* The troops of the first assault wave carry their boats from the forward assembly area to the water under the direction of the engineer crew. The senior engineer crew member, who is in charge of the movement, follows close behind the boat, accompanied by the leader of the infantrymen assigned to the boat. The second engineer soldier acts as guide at the head of the group, near the bow of the boat.

b. The following general rules should be observed during the forward movement:

(1) Not more than ten men attempt to carry the boat at any one time, and not less than four are used for even a short carry.

(2) From the time of its departure from the final assembly area until the moment when the far river bank is reached, the forward movement of each assault boat should be generally uninterrupted. Momentary halts may be made en route to permit the changing of handholds and to avoid detection through movement when flares are dropped; such stops should be few and brief. A short pause must be made at the near edge of the water for the loading of passengers and weapons.

(3) Movement should be by the most direct practicable route to the crossing front; movements along the near bank, or in the water, and parallel to the shore are dangerous and are avoided.

(4) All suitable routes forward from the final assembly area are used; dispersion is essential—the bunching of columns on a few of the more easily traversed routes may be disastrous; route markings and guides (furnished by the engineers) are indispensable.

(5) Movement from the various final assembly areas is timed by the engineer leaders so as to insure that all boats of the first wave are launched at approximately the same moment without delay by any boat at the bank of the river.

(6) The sounds of objects striking the sides or bottoms of the light, hollow hull resound loudly. Great care must be exercised to preserve silence. Nothing whatever should be placed in the boat during the hand carry. Rifles are slung on the shoulders away from the boat side and rifle butts or other equipment are not allowed to come into contact therewith. At the most convenient carrying height the clearance between the bottom of the boat and the ground is not great, and hence every precaution must be taken to avoid striking stumps, rocks, and other obstructions with the boat, and to prevent the bottom from being dropped or dragged on the ground.

148. CROSSING THE RIVER.—*a. Launching and loading.*—(1) Immediately upon arrival at the river bank and without change in the carrying formation, the boat is carried bow first into the water until a depth sufficient to float the fully loaded

boat is reached. Ammunition, machine guns, and any similar weapons or equipment are quietly placed in the boat. Then, and not until then, the passengers move aboard, keeping the boat in balance and avoiding the noise which would certainly be caused by striking any part of the boat with heavy footgear, weapons, or paddles. In shallow water, care must be exercised to prevent grounding the boat, which, with its attendant noise and delay, is particularly dangerous at this time. One engineer soldier stations himself with paddle at the bow; the other, who commands the boat, ascertains that the boat is in balance and that paddlers are properly distributed before climbing aboard himself at the stern and then giving the low command to shove off.

(2) Paddlers, with rifles slung, kneel on the one knee nearer the side of the boat, three paddlers to each side. Other passengers crouch low in the interior of the boat, holding their rifles upright against the floor.

(3) Occasionally, when the water is deep at the bank, the boat may be soundlessly lowered or slid from the bank to the water. The boat is then held parallel to the bank at bow and stern by the engineer crew and loaded directly from the bank.

b. Crossing the water.—(1) Each boat starts across as soon as loaded and proceeds as rapidly as possible by the most direct route to the opposite bank. No attempt should be made to maintain formation of any kind while on the water, although intervals between boats should be preserved to a certain extent. Neither should any effort be made to paddle somewhat upstream in order to counteract drift, unless the relative positions of landing and embarkation points and the nature of the current have led to prior and explicit orders to such effect. Under conditions of complete darkness or of heavy fog or smoke, the proper direction of the boat may be most readily maintained by use of the luminous compass.

(2) Paddlers hold their paddles away from the carrying rail along the gunwales to avoid the sounds of scraping or striking the hull. Splashing is avoided. Passengers do not move about. Firing from the boat is rarely attempted and at night is expressly prohibited.

c. Landing.—(1) *During darkness.*—The boatmen seek to ground the boat in shallow, quiet water and allow the infantrymen to disembark quietly. The infantry leader in the boat instructs his men how and when to get out. Unless the boat is under fire, silence is maintained. The leader orders his men to leave the boat and join him ashore at a designated place (tree, stump, bank, or other easily recognized point). Here, unless attacked or under direct fire, the men lie down and fix bayonets, the leader checks to see that all are there, and then selects an objective for his next movement. He organizes his men into a patrol formation and moves toward the point designated by the platoon or the company commander. If he encounters enemy parties, he attacks at once with the bayonet. He is careful to lead his patrol in such a manner as to avoid collision with friendly troops; senior leaders present organize the patrols to form a platoon organization as soon as possible.

(2) *During daylight.*—The landing is made under protection of combat aviation and artillery fires. Troops disembark rapidly; each boatload moves immediately to join its platoon leader. Once troops are ashore, the procedure is generally the same as in other battle situations.

[…]

152. ATTACK OF VILLAGES.—*a. General.*—(1) If practicable, the village is first enveloped and isolated by the capture of the near and lateral edges. Mopping up of the interior defenses is normally postponed until attacking troops are in position to prevent reinforcements from reaching the defenders. When the village forms part of a main defensive line, reduction of exterior defenses by troops which advance past the flanks of the village facilitates occupation of the lateral edges. Depending upon the situation, the outflanking action may be launched at the same time as the direct attack on the village or may precede it.

(2) When possible, a single unit makes the attack. This unit should be given a zone of action which includes favorable avenues for outflanking the village and the locations from which hostile weapons may place flanking fire in front of the village. The boundary between units should seldom pass along the edge of a village.

b. Outflanking action.—Attacking troops advance past the flanks of the village to a location from which they can place close-range fire upon the outflanked lateral edge, the rear defenses, and any hostile troops in rear of the village. Routes of approach extending to within 300 or 400 yards of the flank or rear of the locality are sought.

c. Capture of lateral edges.—The lateral edge of the village may be captured at the same time as the near edge when the situation and terrain favor a converging attack. Otherwise the exterior rifle units (charged with the capture of the lateral edges) reach positions adjacent to the near edge of the village about the same time as the interior unit (charged with the capture of the near edge). The exterior units then move forward along the lateral edges. Exterior attacking units are disposed in considerable depth and echeloned so as to converge upon the lateral edges of the village. Entrances to the village constitute successive objectives; as each is captured, a garrison is detailed to hold it.

d. Action of interior elements.—(1) The interior action is conducted with minimum forces. These troops first gain a foothold on the forward edge. The advance through the village should be so organized as to maintain cohesion between units and consists of a series of bounds, usually in a single general direction. The principal cross streets constitute objectives near which halts are made to restore contact and cohesion.

(2) Mopping-up troops are usually divided into street and searching detachments and at times into detachments to advance along roofs. Street

detachments advance in single file by small units on both sides of a street. The men on one side watch the windows, cellar gratings, and roofs on the other side. When resistance is encountered, the hostile fire is avoided while detachments seek to reach the enemy's flank and rear. It may be necessary to pierce passageways through the walls of houses and inclosures. Defenders of cellars are reduced by chemicals or incendiary grenades. Houses from which particularly stubborn resistance is offered may be demolished by close-range fire of cannon. Troops progressing along roofs clear out hostile snipers and machine guns and take hostile defenses under fire. Searching parties examine all houses. If night falls before the mopping-up can be completed, it is resumed at daybreak.

e. Fire support.—In the initial stages of the attack, artillery fire is directed against the near and lateral edges of the village, particularly the region of the entrance, and against the weapons outside the village which flank the locality. Groups of houses around central squares or important street crossings are also suitable targets. Tanks are used to neutralize hostile weapons located outside the village and at the edges of the village. They accompany the advance along the lateral edges. A strong infantry base of fire supports the initial attack. Fire support during the combat within the village is limited. Mortars and guns may be employed effectively against defenders of barricades: the artillery action during this period consists principally of incendiary fires and fires on hostile reserves in rear of the village.

CHAPTER 5

COMBAT—LESSONS LEARNED

The *Combat Lessons* series of documents open an invaluable window through which we can see the relationship between frontline experience and training in the U.S. ground forces in World War II. The purpose was to record and disseminate the insights of combat leaders down to junior officers and enlisted men. Note that these were in no way classified documents. The introduction to the series stated:

> The purpose of "Combat Lessons" is to give to our officers and enlisted men the benefit of the battle experiences of others. To be of maximum benefit these lessons must be disseminated *without delay*. They do not necessarily represent the carefully considered views of the War Department; they do, however, reflect the actual experiences of combat and, therefore, merit careful reading. For this reason, also, no single issue can cover many of the phases of combat; lessons will be drawn from the reports as they are received from the theaters of operation and quickly disseminated so that others may apply them. The suggestions which are made or implied are not intended to change the tactical doctrine by which our Army has been trained but rather to elaborate thereon. Much of the subject matter has been covered in training literature, but the comments show that shortcomings continue to manifest themselves on the battlefield.

There is much honesty in this introduction—honesty about the limitations of training, about military bureaucracy (implied), about the difference between theory and practice. But the emphasis on distribution "*without delay*" (the italics are original) illustrates how any considerations about going through the "proper channels" had to be put to one side for the sake of the survivability of the frontline soldier.

The extracts from the series given below—from No. 1 and No. 4 (both 1944)—give tactical information derived from combat experience in Sicily, Italy, and Normandy, plus some additional information from the PTO, which was nonetheless generally applicable to infantry warfare. Much of the advice given is concrete and practical, sometimes brutally so, such as using sheep to clear minefields and applying phosphorus to set fire to the materials the Germans had used to camouflage positions and vehicles. Much is also focused on the best use of various small-arms and support weapons, and it is notable that the bayonet still crops up on several occasions; bayonets had not been entirely consigned to history just yet. At the same time, the frontline commentators also reflect upon the importance of the ageless aspects of human behavior in warfare, such as courage, self-discipline, motivation, and violent intent. Without these, all the weapons in the U.S. infantry were little more than just wood and metal.

From *Combat Lessons No. 1* (1944)

SECTION I
INFANTRY

BATTLE LEADERSHIP

Again and again reports from the battlefields confirm the importance of leadership in every grade, whether it be Corporal or Colonel. Other combat lessons are important; the exercise of leadership in battle is vital. Leadership has often been defined in theory. Here are some instances of its application or its absence on the battlefield. These are but a few examples; there are many others.

* * *

Junior Officer in Battle *Captain William T. Gordon, Infantry, <u>Sicily</u>:* "Since November 8, I have had seventeen officers in my company, and I am the only one who started out with it who is left in the fight. In Tunisia, from troops pinned down in the dark, I have heard enlisted men call out such things as 'Where is an officer to lead us?'—'We don't want to lie here—we want to attack—where is an officer?'… In each case an officer or officers have risen to the occasion, but this nevertheless shows beyond anything else the demand for battle leadership.

"A company officer must build a legend about himself. He must take calculated risks. He must, on the other hand, do what he expects his men to do: he must always dig in; always take cover. His men must know that when he ducks they must duck; on the other hand, they must not believe that when the officer ducks they must run away. The officer must come through every barrage and bombing with a sheepish grin and a wry remark. Masterly understatement of hardship and danger endured plus a grin always pays dividends.

Hate Your Enemy! "Our men do not ordinarily hate. They *must* hate. They are better soldiers when they hate. They must not fraternize with prisoners—must not give them cigarettes and food the moment they are taken. Hate can be taught men by meticulous example. The Rangers are so taught."

* * *

Leaders in Front *Staff Sergeant Richard E. Deland, Infantry, <u>Sicily</u>:* "We want our Captain out front; we don't care much about the position of our battalion commander."

Keep Them Moving! *Operation Report, Seventh Army, <u>Sicily</u>:* "During an attack officers and noncommissioned officers must never allow men to lie prone and passive under enemy fire. They must be required to move forward if this is at all possible.

If movement is absolutely impossible, have the troops at least open fire. The act of firing induces self-confidence in attacking troops; The familiar expression 'Dig or Die' has been greatly overworked. Attacking troops must not be allowed to dig in until they have secured their final objective. If they dig in when momentarily stopped by enemy fire, it will take dynamite to blast them from their holes and resume the advance."

* * *

NCO Leadership *Staff Sergeant Robert J. Kemp, Platoon Sergeant, Infantry, Sicily:* "NCO leadership is important. Leaders, NCOs, and officers should be taken to an OP for terrain instruction and study before an attack. This has been possible in my outfit about one-fourth of the time. We have what is called an 'Orders Group,' which consists of that group of officers and NCOs that must be assembled for instruction before any tactical move."

* * *

Keep Your Mission in Mind! *Lieutenant Colonel E. B. Thayer, Field Artillery, Observer With Fifth Army, Italy:* "Difficulty was experienced in making patrol leaders realize the importance of bringing back information by a specified hour, in time to be of value. Patrols often returned, after encountering resistance, without accomplishing their mission.

Sending them back to accomplish their mission, despite their fatigue, seemed to be the most effective solution to the training problem involved, although the information required often arrived too late."

* * *

Lieutenant Colonel T. F. Bogart, Infantry, Observer With Fifth Army, Italy: "Greater emphasis must be placed on inculcating in junior officers and NCOs the will to accomplish assigned missions despite opposition. A few accounts of patrol actions illustrate this point:

"(1) A reconnaissance patrol consisting of a platoon was sent out at about 1900 one evening to determine the strength if any of the Germans in two small towns, the first about two miles away and the second about three miles farther on. The patrol reached the outskirts of the first town and met an Italian. who told them there were no Germans in the town and then started to lead the patrol into town. A few hundred yards farther on a German machine gun opened up, the Italian disappeared, three of the patrol were killed, and the others dispersed. They drifted back to our battalion during the night, and it was not until nearly daylight that the practically valueless report of the action was received. Not the slightest conception of the strength in the first town was obtained and no information of the second town. It was necessary to send out another patrol with the same mission.

"(2) A patrol was sent out with the mission of determining the condition of a road, especially bridges, over a three-mile stretch to the front. When this patrol had covered about a mile it ran into a motorized German patrol. Two of the Americans were killed, and the platoon leader claimed six Germans. The patrol leader forgot his mission, returned to the battalion CP with the remainder of his patrol, and had to be sent out again with a great loss in time in getting the information desired.

"(3) On several occasions patrols were sent out on reconnaissance missions with instructions to get certain information by a specific time. The hour would pass and sometimes several others without a word from the patrol. Sometimes it was due to difficulties encountered, sometimes to mistakes in computation of time and space factors, but in all cases there was no good reason why some information did not get back by the specified time."

COMMENT: The failure of patrols in these instances stems from a lack of appreciation on the part of NCOs and junior officers of their <u>missions</u>. In patrol actions, as in the operations of larger units, the <u>mission</u> must he kept uppermost in the minds of all ranks, and no action should be undertaken which does not contribute directly to the accomplishment of that mission. Conversely, no incidental or inadvertent contact with the enemy should deter or divert patrols from the complete accomplishment of their missions, to include compliance with <u>all</u> instructions given, where humanly possible.

Team Up! *Captain William, T. Gordon, Infantry, <u>Sicily</u>:* "I have found that men in position must fight in pairs; an order that 50 per cent stay awake is thus easily enforced; it bolsters morale and nerves.

Rally Point "In every company attack order a reserve force must be prescribed; I always do even though sometimes this force consists only of myself and my First Sergeant. Often a soldier who a moment before has run away is converted into a fighter by leadership. A reserve force gives him a rallying point."

* * *

Fear is Normal *Colonel George Taylor, Infantry, <u>Sicily</u>:* "Fear of being afraid is the greatest obstacle for the new man in battle to overcome. There is no reason for shame in being afraid. Men who have had excellent battle records freely admit they are scared stiff in battle. The important thing is that every soldier must be taught all he needs to know so well that battlefield thinking is reduced to a minimum; automatic, disciplined reactions to battlefield problems must be the rule.

"In battle the worst element is mental and nervous exhaustion. There is no real rest under fire. The ability to withstand fire is more important than all the knowledge in the world."

U.S. soldiers of the 10th Mountain Division cover an assault squad attacking Germans in a building in Italy, March 1945.

SICILY—ITALY—ATTU

NIGHT ATTACK

Surprise Saves Lives *Major John R. Patterson, Infantry, Sicily:* "The mission of our battalion after landing south of GELA in Sicily was to capture the airport at BISCARI. The battalion used the silent night attack. The three rifle companies were in line with the heavy-weapons company in reserve. To reach its line of departure, the battalion crossed two precipitous ridges using two control lines, then climbed the cliff at the airport to the line of departure. All this was done silently under cover of darkness.

"The attack was started with a hand grenade. We didn't fire until the Germans counterattacked. We went in with bayonets and hand grenades and caught some of the Germans undressed and dressing. The MK IV tanks fired their guns but wouldn't close on us. The enemy knew their men were all about, so fired their machine guns and rifles mainly into the air.

"The first counterattack came in two hours, and there was one about each hour thereafter until 1600. They had all emplacements wired and fixed with trip-wire booby traps. We removed the traps and used the emplacements during counterattacks.

"We found a line of airplane bombs wired to blow up the area; we de-activated them. A German plane landed just as we were ready to leave the line of departure. Later, one of our men grenaded it.

"The battalion took no transportation. I had with me the S-3, one runner, and one 511 radio [a 20lb, battery-operated, short-range transmitter-receiver]. The wire came up thirty minutes later, but was not necessary. I estimate the enemy had a reinforced battalion. His tanks and self-propelleds came up later. Some of the enemy were air personnel, and there were about eleven AA guns set up for antipersonnel use.

"Our attack lasted thirty minutes. We had no casualties during the attack; two were killed during the counterattacks."

* * *

Hand-to-Hand Fighting *Captain Jarrold, Infantry:* "At BISCARI AIRPORT I used my trench knife twice. One of my men got three with his bayonet. He shot one, then another tried to grab his bayonet. He got this one with the bayonet. That got him started, so he got three in all before it was over.

Small Arms Against Armor "We found that caliber .30 AP pierces enemy armored half-tracks at close ranges."

* * *

Platoon Action *Lieutenant Hollerich, Infantry:* "Company A, moving forward in darkness to participate in the BISCARI AIRPORT fight, ran right into the enemy position. Before the fight started, my platoon crossed the road just above a culvert and reached the south edge of the airport, but I was ordered to take it back to a position just east of the culvert. I wish I could have stayed where I was because it was a perfect place from which to envelop the resistance in front of my company.

"When the enemy machine guns opened up we threw grenades. The machine guns pulled back out of grenade fire. Then NCOs and Browning Automatic Riflemen went up over the embankment, through and beyond the initial enemy positions. Eventually we had a base of fire of about twenty men including the BARs.

"During the enemy counterattacks we did pretty well with other fire, too. Lead was flying fast and furiously at twenty to thirty yards. We fire at flashes. In this kind of firing *you learn to fire and roll to one side or they'll soon get you.*

"One of the corporals sneaked up on a dug-in vehicle and got it with an '03 rifle grenade at 25 yards.

"The 'bazooka' man of my platoon heard 'Tanks to the right,' went around a bend in the road, and fired at about 35 yards. He got the first of a pair of vehicles.

A German officer tried to capture him with a pistol, but he gave the officer an uppercut and then killed him with his helmet. I don't know how the other vehicle was knocked out, but one of the BAR men got its driver."

COMMENT: In these accounts of a successful night attack by a small unit the application of the following principles is worthy of note:

a. **Close control during the approach by the use of control lines adjusted to difficult terrain features.**

b. **Designation of a Line of Departure as close to the objective as possible and after all major terrain obstacles had been passed. This is essential to assure proper organization of the unit immediately prior to the assault.**

c. **Attainment of the vital element of surprise (Germans caught undressed and dressing, airplanes landing on the field).**

d. **Use of the bayonet and hand grenades with no weapon firing permitted. It may often be advisable to prohibit the loading of rifles.**

e. **Use of frontal attack only. Any attempt at envelopment tends to cause disorder and confusion. Note that one platoon which had advanced ahead of the general line was pulled back to conform.**

f. **A definite and limited objective—capture of an airfield, in this case— in which the entire front could be covered by manpower rather than fire- power. These are the major elements of a successful night attack brought out in the foregoing account. Others not mentioned but which were undoubtedly contributing factors in this operation are:**

Careful planning in minute detail.

Precise, specific orders.

Careful arrangements for maintenance of direction.

Thorough daylight reconnaissance by as many of the leaders as possible.

Use of compact columns in the approach formation until the Line of Departure is reached.

KNOCKING OUT PILLBOXES

Colonel Rogers, Infantry, <u>Sicily</u>: "The neutralization and reduction of concrete pillboxes played an important part in the Sicilian campaign. In the initial landing phases alone, this regiment cleaned out over thirty of these pillboxes. They were located all over the place as we went inland.

"They were cleverly constructed and elaborately camouflaged. Many were covered with brush, grass, straw, or other natural stuff. Others had cane houses built over them to represent peasant outbuildings or huts. All those we encountered in and about villages and towns were covered over with some kind of house to conceal them. Most of these were cane or wood shacks, though some were actually covered with plaster or stucco to represent real houses. Many had dummy houses built right over the pillbox, and windows arranged to give full freedom of fire from the embrasures of the pillbox inside the shell of the building. In the open country a number were also built with hay ricks and straw stacks over them, all very natural and innocent looking.

"Reduction of these often proved very simple, and in many cases the enemy simply dug his own grave in his efforts at camouflage. When we learned not to be surprised by them and recognized them for what they were, we developed a very simple method of dealing with the ones concealed by straw, hay, cane, and other inflammable material. We dosed them freely with white phosphorus, especially from the attached chemical mortars, and this did the work to perfection. We set the camouflage on fire, blinded the gunners inside, and choked them with the phosphorus and the smoke from the burning hay, straw, and other material. The fire and heat, too, made the interiors untenable, and the occupants would become terrified and come out and surrender in a bunch.

"In one place near LICATA there were several of these straw- and hay-covered pillboxes, also some concealed with cane huts, arranged at key positions in country covered with wheat fields and terraced grain plantings. We simply set a first-class prairie fire with our white phosphorus, and burned out a position over 2,500 yards long. We waited until the wind was right and let them have it. Every pillbox was burned out. The more difficult pillboxes that wouldn't burn we attacked with massed fire from mortars of all types, AT guns, and heavy machine guns. In the case of very tough ones that were reinforced, we used 'bazooka' rockets and at times sent men up close under heavy covering fire and knocked them out with bangalore torpedoes."

COMMENT: The use of fire is, of course, dependent on favorable weather conditions. Careful coordination is also necessary to insure that the resulting smoke does not interfere with the operations and observation of adjacent units.

[…]

INFANTRY WEAPONS

IN JUNGLE WARFARE

The following comments on the use and effectiveness of infantry weapons in jungle warfare appear in the report of the 43d Division on the MUNDA Campaign—NEW GEORGIA:

Basic Weapons "The M1 rifle is doubtless the best all-around weapon possessed by our troops. Its serviceability under existing campaign conditions is excellent. Ammunition supply was adequate, since the rifle was normally fired only at observed targets. The Japs possessed a number of our M1 rifles, apparently considering them a superior weapon to their own.

"The fragmentation grenade was used frequently against suspected areas of heavy jungle growth and on some occasions for the destruction of booby traps around perimeter defenses. Its effect when used as a booby trap is questionable because of the long fuze time. *The Japs used our grenades extensively in their night harassing raids against our bivouacs.* Rifle grenades were used on some occasions with success against enemy pillboxes.

"In spite of its handicap of sounding like a Jap .25-caliber light machine gun, the Thompson sub-machine gun proved very satisfactory for specialized personnel such as linemen, artillery forward observers, vehicle drivers, and reconnaissance personnel. Its limited range made it especially useful in combat in rear areas.

"The Browning auto rifle gave excellent service. This weapon has high jungle mobility and provides excellent fire power for the short-range targets frequently encountered. It has been used many times to reinforce the final protective lines at night, to establish trail blocks, to cover patrol advances, and to destroy snipers.

"The light machine gun proved very effective in the night security of bivouacs. At other times, it was used to cover the advance of attacking echelons by placing heavy fire in the direction of suspected pillboxes. Since fields of fire and visibility were so limited the effectiveness of such support was questionable.

"We did not use the heavy machine gun to any extent in the attack in the jungle. This was mainly due to its weight and to its heavy ammunition supply requirements. It was used primarily for the defense of beachheads and water passageways, also to some extent in the defense of regimental and battalion command posts.

"The 60mm mortar was not effective against enemy pillboxes, although it unquestionably contributed by its demoralizing effect on the enemy. After we reached the outer taxiways of the airfield, we had excellent visibility from ideally situated OPs, and the disorganized enemy presented many profitable targets for this weapon. *The exceptional accuracy of the weapon made it very valuable in close support, and its use during the assault on the revetments and shell craters at* MUNDA FIELD *and* KOKENGOLO HILL *is credited with saving many lives.*

"The 81mm mortar proved to be one of the most important single weapons contributing to the success of this offensive. Because of the difficulty of supply only two mortars were taken forward with each heavy-weapons company, the balance of the personnel being used as ammunition carriers. Troops frequently remarked that if given the choice of rations or 81mm mortar ammunition, they would gladly take the latter.

"While the 37mm AT gun is admittedly a weapon of opportunity in jungle warfare, there were two occasions on which it served us handsomely. The Nips had a field piece located where it could interdict our beachhead at LAIANA. Scouts located the gun, but our mortar fire couldn't silence it. We disassembled a 37mm gun and carried it forward under cover of the dense foliage. The gun was then assembled under cover and moved rapidly to a point in the open from where it could command the target. *Three accurately aimed rounds destroyed the gun and killed its crew.*

"On another occasion we picked up an enemy occupied pillbox about 600 yards from one of our OPs. The 37mm gun was manhandled to a position on the forward slope in only partial concealment. It placed accurate and intense fire on the pillbox and completely destroyed it.

"The value of the 37mm gun was also proved by two episodes when the enemy attempted to make night landings. First, one enemy barge was fired on as it neared a landing on BOMBOE PENINSULA. Both HE and AP ammunition were used, and the barge was heard to limp away, sputtering badly. On another night a group of Japs approached the north coast of SAGEKARASAS ISLAND in an assault boat. Antitank gunners held their fire until the boat was nearly ashore, then fired several rounds of canister. The boat was seen to sink and several bodies floated ashore the next day.

4.2" Chemical Mortar "The 4.2-inch chemical mortar company was placed under the control of the Division Artillery and the fires of the chemical mortars coordinated with artillery fires. These mortars, employing a 25-pound high-explosive shell, were used successfully with the artillery in firing preparations prior to an attack and in firing prearranged fires such as area barrages to block enemy routes and to disrupt barge traffic near WESTERN SAGEKARASAS ISLAND. One prisoner stated that the mortar barrages were more feared by them than artillery. The only criticism of the weapon is that the shell has no delayed fuze; consequently, a great many tree bursts result from its use."

* * *

IN SICILY

Advance Guard *Captain Reed, Infantry:* "We have had considerable success in using a platoon of heavy machine guns with each advance or assault company. You need this increase of fire power right up there in front. With the advance guard we put a platoon of machine guns right up in the forward support. We also put a section of 37mm AT guns right behind the advance party. The remaining section of AT guns is placed behind the support of the advance guard. We place the 57mm's and the cannon company in the center of the main body."

U.S. combat patrol engages German machine-gun nest near Lucca, Italy, 1944.

* * *

Pyrotechnics *Staff Sergeant Robert, J. Kemp, Infantry:* "We want lots of pyrotechnics for use in all kinds of situations to include bedeviling the enemy. Sometimes Jerry puts on a pyrotechnic show that just scares hell out of us; it would work on him too."

* * *

Miscellaneous Comment *Various Small Infantry Unit Commanders:* "81mm mortar: A perfect weapon. I like to use the alternate traversing method.

"60mm mortar: We kept them right up in front and used them of ten.

"Bazooka: We have had no trouble with our bazookas. Have gotten several tanks with them.

"37mm AT gun: Very mobile. It's artillery; good against anything—vehicles, pillboxes, personnel, houses. Gets in faster than the mortar. If I had to throw away any heavy weapons, the '37' would be the last to go.

"75mm self-propelled cannon: Excellent for coordinated attack—perfect. Too vulnerable to get very close initially."

* * *

AT SALERNO

The "Bazooka" Worked *Operations report, __th Infantry:* "Several tank attacks occurred which the Infantry fought off with their 'bazookas.' It became more and more apparent that this was really an effective weapon. During this one day it destroyed seven enemy tanks."

COMMENT: Numerous reports indicate the effectiveness of the "Bazooka" when used by trained personnel. It has been used successfully against pillboxes, machine-gun nests, and personnel.

[...]

INFANTRY–TANK TEAM

Opportunity Lost *Captain Putnam, Infantry, Sicily:* "The infantry should be given practical training in cooperation with tanks. I don't mean the armored infantry— they're part of the armored division and work with them all the time. I mean ordinary infantry like us. I know our regiment didn't have any training with tanks in preparation for combat. At BRANIERI we just didn't know how to work with the attached tank unit. When our tanks came up to support us after we had broken up the German attack, we did not follow up the tanks properly as they went forward. Had we done so we could have cleaned out almost a battalion of Germans. We had not been trained to work with tanks, and we remained in position after they went forward. If we had known how to go forward with them: we could have done a much better job and could have gotten all of the Germans' vehicles and materiel. After this experience, we strongly recommend that all infantry be given practical training in cooperation with tanks in action. Get the infantrymen used to tanks and how to fight together with them."

Lesson Learned *First Marine Division, Guadalcanal:* "The initial assault by our five tanks across the field east of our 3d Battalion lines at the 'Battle of Bloody Ridge' on GUADALCANAL was entirely successful. They caused much havoc among the enemy and returned unharmed. Within an hour, they attacked again over the same terrain. Meanwhile, the Japs had had time to move 37mm AT guns into position along the edge of the woods at the eastern side of the field. These guns knocked out three of our tanks during the second assault. It thus proved extremely unwise to launch a second attack over the same route. and terrain. This is especially true if there is sufficient elapsed time for the enemy to move AT guns into position."

Infantry-Tank Attack *Lieutenant Colonel Perkins, Tank Battalion Commander, Italy:* "Shortly after landing at SALERNO we attacked a hill south of the town of OLIVETO. The attack was up a winding road. The medium tanks moved down into the bottoms at the foot of the hill into a covered position and covered the light tanks as they went up. As the light tanks went up the hill both the lights and mediums fired on the enemy infantry. When they spotted enemy soldiers going into buildings the mediums took care of the buildings, leaving the light tanks to take care of the infantry and the machine guns. Both the lights and mediums stayed until the infantry took over. 'The 'rush-to-battle' idea is wrong. Here we creep up. Each tank should overwatch another tank; each section should overwatch another section; each platoon another platoon."

From *Combat Lessons No.4* **(1944)**

SECTION II
NORMAL OPERATIONS

FIGHTING IN NORMANDY

Bucking the Hedgerows The terrain in the area selected for the initial penetration of French soil was generally level or gently sloping. However, it was broken up into a "crazy quilt" pattern of small fields separated by "hedgerows." These consisted of an earthen mound or wall 8 to 10 feet in width and 4 to 6 feet in height, covered with a scrub undergrowth.

Along the top of this wall grew rows of trees. Forming an important part of the obstacle thus created was the ditch which ran along one or both sides of the mound. The roads, narrow and winding, ran between these hedgerows, and offered the defenders many advantageous positions for ambuscades or surprise attacks on advancing foot-troops and armor. Observation was normally limited from one hedgerow to the next, although an occasional structure, such as the church tower in a village would widen the horizon.

These peculiarities of terrain led to the development of special operational techniques in the application of tactical principles. Quoted below are some experience reports, from the battlefield, of hedgerow fighting.

The German Defense Ever since August 1940 the Germans have been studying and organizing the beach defenses of. the French coast. They are past masters of the art of utilizing the terrain to advantage.

As set forth in a letter from the *Commanding General, U.S. XIX Corps:* "The Germans have been thorough in their defense. Their weapons are normally sited to provide long fields of fire. The 88-mm dual purpose gun, the 'Tiger' tank with its 88-mm gun, or the 'Panther' tank which has a 75-mm high-velocity gun, normally takes you under fire at ranges up to 2,000 yards. All weapons are well dug in. The mobility of their tanks is often sacrificed in order to secure the protection of a ditch or the walls of a building.

Sniper Trouble "The German soldiers had been given orders to stay in their positions and, unless you rooted them out, they would stay, even though your attack had passed by or over them. Some of their snipers stayed hidden for 2 to 5 days after a position had been taken and then 'popped up' suddenly with a rifle or AT grenade launcher to take the shot for which they had been waiting.

"We found fire crackers with slow burning fuse left by snipers and AT gun crews in their old positions when they moved. These exploded at irregular intervals, giving the impression that the position was still occupied by enemy forces.

"High losses among tank commanders have been caused by German snipers. Keep buttoned up, as the German rifleman concentrates on such profitable targets. This is especially true in villages. After an action the turret of the commander's tank is usually well marked with rifle bullets.

Enemy in Ambush "On several occasions the Germans have allowed small patrols of ours to enter villages and wander around unmolested, but when stronger forces were sent forward to occupy the village they would encounter strong resistance. The Germans will permit a patrol to gather erroneous information in order to ambush the follow-up troops acting on the patrol's false report."

German Weapons One infantry regimental commander has given a good detailed description of the defensive organization: "We found that the enemy employed very

U.S. infantry engaged in street fighting in Germany, 1945.

few troops with an extremely large number of automatic weapons. All personnel and automatic weapons were well dug in along the hedgerows in excellent firing positions. In most cases the approaches to these positions were covered by mortar fire. Also additional fire support was provided by artillery field pieces of 75-mm, 88-mm, and 240-mm caliber firing both time and percussion fire. Numerous snipers located in trees, houses, and towers were used.

Our Attack "The most successful method of dealing with these defensive positions was the closely coordinated attack of infantry and tanks, with artillery and 4.2-inch chemical mortars ready to assist where needed. The use of these supporting weapons was severely handicapped by the limited observation."

* * *

TANK–INFANTRY COMBINE

Teamwork the Key The great emphasis placed on the importance of tank–infantry teamwork is reflected in the many reports and training instructions that have been issued by combat commanders. For example, the *Commanding General, VII Corps* published the following narrative of such an action in a training memorandum: "The capture of the high ground north of the MONTEBOURG–QUINEVILLE ROAD was accomplished by the 3d Battalion, 22d Infantry, closely supported by the 70th Tank Battalion, which was operating at a reduced strength of 18 tanks.

"Upon receiving the order for the attack at 1830, 13 June, the tank battalion commander immediately initiated a route reconnaissance to a suitable assembly area and arranged for a conference between his key officers and those of the infantry battalion.

Elements of the Plan "At this conference the following essential elements to effect coordination were agreed upon:

"1. H-hour would be at 0930.

"2. An artillery preparation would be fired from H-15 minutes to H-hour.

"3. When the artillery fire lifted, the tank mortar platoon, from positions immediately in rear of the Line of Departure, would fire on all known and suspected AT gun locations.

"4. Each of the two infantry assault companies would be directly supported by six tanks. The remaining six tanks would, be in general support.

"5. All tanks would be held 800 yards in rear of the LD [Line of Departure], moving forward in time to cross the line with the infantry at H-hour.

The Advance "The attack jumped off on time, the tanks advancing very slowly, spraying the hedgerows with machine-gun fire. The infantry advanced abreast of the tanks, mopping up as they proceeded. The supporting tank company remained about 500 to 600 yards in rear of the assault companies and covered their forward movement by overhead fire.

"The objective was seized at 1500 after an advance of over 2,000 yards against a well-organized resistance which utilized both open and concrete emplacements."

Corp Commander's Comment: In discussing this attack the Corps Commander made the following comments on infantry–tank cooperation:

"Tank companies require at least 3 hours and tank battalions a minimum of 5 hours of daylight in which to prepare for an attack.

"Tank assembly positions should be selected well in rear of the Line of Departure.

"Tank officers and infantry commanders. should discuss and arrange all details of their cooperative effort by personal conference at some prearranged location. If possible this location should allow visual reconnaissance of the zone of activity.

"The tanks should not be advanced to the LD until the time of the attack.

"Artillery observers should be with the leading wave of tanks.

"Radio communication between the infantry CP and the tanks should be maintained.

"The speed of the tanks should conform to the infantry rate of advance. Gaps should not be allowed to develop between the two elements.

"The infantry can assist the tanks in passing through hedgerows by protecting them from hostile AT personnel using AT grenades or rockets.

"In the absence of definite targets forward infantry elements should fire at the nearest cover to the front and flanks. Rifle fire directed along the lower structures of friendly tanks will discourage enemy use of magnetic mines.

"Enemy AT guns firing at our tanks should be immediately smothered by our mortar and automatic-weapons fire, thus forcing the gun crews to take cover and permitting the tanks to outflank and destroy the enemy guns.

"Tanks should be employed on both sides of hedges when advancing along a hedgerow.

"If at all possible tanks should avoid roads during the attack.

"The tanks in general support should mop up any positions which are bypassed by the first wave of tanks.

"Once the final objective is reached the tanks should immediately withdraw to a predetermined rally point. If they remain with the infantry they will attract heavy enemy artillery fire which will seriously interfere with the infantry reorganization."

* * *

Limited Objectives A letter from *Headquarters, XIX Corps*, stresses the importance of the limited objective in controlling the combined infantry–tank action: "The major objective given in corps, division, and even regimental plans and orders is reached by a series of limited-objective attacks by infantry and tank platoons and companies. Thus the designation of the major objective should be considered as indicating an axis of advance and an ultimate goal for the smaller assault units. Here in NORMANDY the normal objective of each attack is the next hedgerow where there will be a pause for reorganization and for planning the next advance. Keep the distance to be traversed short so that the tanks will not outstrip the infantry, thus losing the close support that is mutually necessary to make the fight effective. It is very desirable whenever conditions permit that each limited objective be visible from the line of departure.

Personal Reconnaissance "The closely coordinated team play that is called for in hedgerow fighting requires a maximum of personal reconnaissance. The key to success in each fight from hedgerow to hedgerow is personal reconnaissance by the commanders concerned."

* * *

Bulldozer Tanks An infantry battalion commander wrote from NORMANDY: "The light and medium tank equipped with a bulldozer blade was successfully used to plow through the hedgerows, cutting openings through which the other tanks would file to fan out and cover the next field. The steep banks which line the roads would be cut down at predetermined crossing points."

* * *

Fighting Infantry *Regimental Commander,* NORMANDY: "Fire and movement is still the only sound way to advance your infantry in daylight fighting. Build up a good strong base of fire with automatic rifles and light machine guns. The heavy machine guns are much more effective, but it is difficult to keep them up with the advance. Use your 60-mm mortars to deepen and thicken your covering fire. When you are all set, cut loose with all you've got to keep Jerry's head down while the riflemen close in from the flanks and clean him out.

Hedgerow Hints "Because of the limited range of observation, scouts tended to operate too close to their units. They should try to keep at least one hedgerow ahead of the remainder of the squad.

"Riflemen still have a tendency to wait for a definite, visible target before shooting. Each man should cover with fire any assigned sector which he believes occupied. Only then will he provide the needed protection to his comrades on the move.

"Avoid the areas in the vicinity of large trees when digging in. Enemy artillery fire in these trees will cause tree bursts with the same effect as time fire."

* * *

Hedgerow Explosives *Observer's Report,* NORMANDY: "The engineers played their part in the tank–infantry team. The sketches show graphically how the closely coordinated tank–infantry–engineer team worked in one of our divisions.

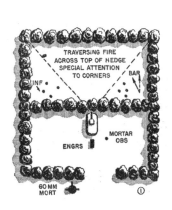

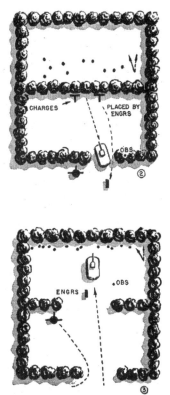

"The tank would place covering fire on the far hedge from a position behind the hedge to be breached. Under this fire the infantry would move into the field ahead to cover the engineer operations. The engineers would place explosive charges to breach the hedge during the infantry advance.

"When the tank fire had to stop to avoid endangering our own infantry, the tank would momentarily withdraw, and the charges would be detonated. The team would then move forward to the next hedgerow to repeat the performance. It was found that two charges of 50 pounds each placed as shown were adequate to breach any type of hedgerow."

* * *

Lean on the Artillery Preparation *Commanding General, 79th Division,* NORMANDY: "Heavy artillery preparation fires, terrifically expensive in ammunition, have been wasted because they were not closely followed up by the attacking infantry. Remember these supporting fires do not destroy the enemy but merely force him underground for a brief period. You must be on top of him when he 'pops up' again."

* * *

The Useful 4.2 *Infantry Battalion Commander,* NORMANDY: "The 4.2-inch chemical mortar has proved to be a wonderful close-support weapon. Captured prisoners stated that they feared it more than artillery shell because they could not hear the projectile. The Germans have shown a marked dislike for WP, and on many occasions a few rounds thrown in their hedgerow positions have caused their precipitate withdrawal.

"We fired the mortars like artillery pieces, using forward observers with the assault rifle companies. The mortars did their best work at ranges of 1,500 to 2,000 yards, but on occasion they have done deadly execution at 3,500 yards."

Battlefield Recovery Under Fire *Letter, First U.S. Army Group,* NORMANDY: "A tank battalion used the following procedure to recover one of their tanks which had been immobilized only 200 yards from the German lines:

"An infantry platoon was placed in concealment in the hedgerow facing the German position and disposed so that its fire would cover the disabled tank. An 81-mm mortar was emplaced on the right flank of the infantry platoon. Then the tank recovery vehicle (T-2) started forward. Almost immediately a German machine gun opened fire but was silenced in short order by the mortar.

"When the recovery vehicle reached the disabled tank, the German infantry opened fire and moved forward, but the heavy fire from our infantry platoon, coupled with a concentration from the mortar, caused their precipitate retirement.

U.S. infantry engage German troops around Bastogne during the German Ardennes Offensive, 1944–45.

The recovery vehicle hooked on to the tank and towed it to safety with no further difficulty and no casualties."

* * *

AIR SUPPORT IN FRANCE

Close Support by Fighter Planes The following incident as related by an observer in FRANCE illustrates the close support which fighter planes have been giving the ground troops in recent fighting in France:

"It was an early morning mission. The planes were to assist the march of one of our armored columns, which was moving rapidly southward. As the planes appeared overhead the following radio conversation took place:

"Ground to plane: 'Hello Kismet Red. This is Bronco. What have you in sight overhead? We have no targets now. Is there anything in those woods off to the left or over the brow of the hill ahead?'

"Five minutes later the plane reports: 'Bronco this is Kismet Red. Don't see anything in the woods and there is nothing over the hill. There are 12 Tiger tanks retreating about 4 miles down the road. Shall we bomb them?'

"The answer comes back, 'Yes, go ahead and bomb them. Save some of your bombs if you can.'

Tank Trap "The P-47s caught the tanks in a ravine, and blasted the leading tank on their first pass. The others, not able to continue on or turn around, were caught in a trap. The planes made repeated passes at very low altitude and destroyed them all.

"As the tank column proceeded it received artillery fire from a patch of woods about 2 miles distant to the left. Since the airplanes couldn't identify the target the tanks marked it with a 75-mm red smoke shell. The squadron unloaded all their bombs on the target and the artillery fire ceased.

The Surrender "The planes continued to cover the column on its march, and about 10 minutes later spotted eight hostile tanks approaching on a road which ran at right angles to the route of the friendly armor. After reporting to the column commander the planes proceeded to strafe the enemy tanks with machine-gun fire until their ammunition was almost exhausted. A 'Jeep' detached itself from the American column and approached the German tanks. When it neared them the tank crews crawled out in haste to surrender.

"This is the type of help the planes are giving. The ground force officers that I talked to were uniform in their praise of the close support fighters."

Antiaircraft in Combat *Colonel W.H. Goodrich, Observer*, FRANCE: "Our complete air superiority has resulted in little activity for the antiaircraft artillery in its primary role. However, several secondary missions have been developed such as antitank fires, field. artillery fires, etc. A most successful employment has been its use in hedgerow fighting. The 90-mm gun has proven its ability to blast through the earthen embankment and dig out the enemy infantry and artillery entrenched behind it.

"The rapid, slashing attack of our infantry and armor has bypassed many enemy centers of resistance. This has resulted in bringing many antiaircraft artillery units in close contact with the enemy. Much of the reconnaissance and occupation of positions has been done under small-arms fire from snipers and small enemy combat groups. The training which a number of units had received in combat infantry technique has proven very useful."

* * *

FIGHTING IN ITALY

Notes from the Beachhead *Monthly Operations Reports of Infantry Regiments, 3d Division,* ANZIO: "Troops remaining for long periods in a defensive situation tend to lose the zest for combat and the aggressive spirit required for successful operations. One corrective measure was to send out 'shoot 'em up' squads. The squads were sent out until contact was made, at which time they would fire all of their ammunition and then withdraw. Also frequent periods of rotation to training areas are recommended.

"A lack of will to employ basic infantry weapons against enemy within range has been noted. All too frequently officers call for supporting artillery and other supporting fire without employing infantry fire power under their immediate control.

"A more thorough understanding of the use of supporting artillery is desirable among infantry officers and noncommissioned officers. They should all know how to adjust artillery and mortar fire.

Morale "The maintenance of high morale in units committed to action for long continuous periods requires the constant attention of leaders. One solution was to establish a regimental rest area in the vicinity of the field train bivouac. Here showers and clean clothes were made available, as well as hot meals. Writing paper, reading material, radios and phonograph records were supplied. The men were sent back in small groups from each company on the line. After having been confined to foxholes by day and to limited movement at night, a 48-hour stay at this rest area improved the morale of the personnel immeasurably."

COMMENT: The methods outlined above, to promote fighting efficiency can be carried out by units of regimental and battalion size by the exercise of resourcefulness and ingenuity on the part of unit commanders.

* * *

WHEN ON PATROL keep your mission in mind. Don't be sidetracked.

IT TAKES the proper amount of water and plenty of time to soak, together with thorough stirring, to reconstitute dehydrated foods.

Unpopular Visitors *Lieutenant Colonel Schull, Commander Armored Regiment,* ANZIO: "Stay away from observation posts and forward command posts unless your business is urgent. More than one good OP or CP has been knocked out because of careless or unnecessary visitors. 'Adding materially to the harrassing efforts of the enemy' (to quote a battalion commander), there has been a constant stream of visitors from all echelons of command but mainly unengaged staff officers of higher headquarters. These visitors, plus the normal traffic of messengers, aid the enemy materially in locating the OP or CP, as well as prevent the personnel from getting any rest during quiet periods of the action.

"It is suggested that more reliance be placed on normal channels of communication and systems of liaison officers at CPs in an effort to reduce the milling mobs of visitors that infest these installations now."

* * *

Fire Fighting with Tankdozers "After suffering high casualties to personnel and equipment while fighting fires in ammunition dumps, an Engineer fire-fighting unit, assisted by an Armored Engineer Battalion, developed a method of combating these fires, 'utilizing an experimental tankdozer fabricated by the Armored Engineer Battalion.

"When the ammunition stacks were above ground the firemen would initially attack the fire with their regular apparatus until the ammunition started to explode. Then the tankdozer would move in and 'bulldoze' the exploding ammunition away from the remainder of the stack, spreading the boxes out and banking earth around and over them. Even when this failed to extinguish the fires, it would cut them down sufficiently to permit the regular fire fighters to continue their operations.

"It was found that when the ammunition stacks were dug in, leaving earth banks beside the stacks, the tankdozer could handle the fire alone. It would push the earth banks on top of the stacks of ammunition, thus smothering the fire.

"In combating a salvage-dump fire, the tankdozer was profitably used to throw up an earth embankment close to the fire. This provided protection for firemen handling hose lines."

* * *

Silent Security A simple alarm device has been improvised in the Mediterranean Theater to assist in providing night security.

It can be readily made up by troops in the field from standard issue materials.

The device is designed to set off two Verey lights in succession. Both are installed on wooden stakes. They are fired by a trip wire which activates the striker mechanisms of two percussion igniters (both of which are on the first stake). One sets off the first Verey light. The other ignites a safety fuse leading to the second Verey light on the other stake. The length of this fuse determines the interval between the flares. The time lag between the two lights should be long enough to allow an enemy patrol to get back on their feet by the time the second light is fired. The activating trip wire should be stretched across likely avenues of patrol movement.

By gauging direction from the first light, troops can prepare to direct their fire in the right direction when the second light illuminates the enemy.

* * *

Animated Mine Exploders *Major Luther J. Reid, Observer* ITALY: "A herd of sheep, hurriedly bought up around the local countryside in ITALY, was used effectively by the 36th Division Engineers in clearing an area on the south bank of the RAPIDO RIVER of the Schu mines that had been planted there in great numbers by retreating Germans.

"The mined area was under direct small-arms fire of the enemy. The only apparent method of clearing a path through it was to send men in at night with steel rods to crawl along on their hands and knees and locate each mine by probing every inch of the ground. This was too slow.

Wanted: 300 Sheep "The engineering officer asked the division quartermaster to provide 300 live sheep. These were made available the next day. Two Engineer officers and an enlisted man disguised themselves as native Italian sheepherders and started driving the flock across the mine field. Near the end of the field, after a number of mines had been detonated, the Germans got wise to the ruse and opened fire, the sheepherders taking cover and withdrawing to safety. But the sheep continued to mill around in the area exploding many mines. The project was considered successful as it provided the necessary cleared path to the riverbank."

Rifle Grenade Grapnel Aids in Creating Tripwires A rifle-projected grapnel, devised by a unit in ETO and constructed from a disarmed Antitank Rifle Grenade M9A1, facilitates the clearance of mine trip wires in open fields while permitting the maximum use of individual cover. Using the rifle grenade launcher, the grapnel may be projected 75 to 100 yards from a covered position. It is then pulled back along the ground by means of an attached cord and the process repeated.

The range of the grenade grapnel, much greater than that of a hand-thrown grapnel, makes possible the clearance of a large area from a single firing position. In confined spaces the grenade grapnel may be hand thrown.

Details of Construction An AT Rifle Grenade M9A1 is stripped of the nose, powder charge, firing mechanism, percussion cap, and booster charge. Three 4-in. common spikes, bent to an approximation of the desired curve, are inserted through holes previously bored at equal distances around the circumference of the body. With 1 inch of each spikehead remaining inside, a wooden plug is driven into the grenade body, forcing the spikes into the plug and binding them in place.

The shaping of the spikes is then completed and the points are rounded off. A wood screw inserted through another hole bored in the body keeps the block from loosening. Immersion in water will cause the wood to swell, giving additional binding effect on the spikes. If facilities are available, hooks may be forged and welded to a disarmed grenade.

A 1½-ft. length of cable wire is passed through the fin assembly and attached to the grenade by means of a loop of soft wire threaded through the safety-pin hole. Approximately 150 yards of trailing cord (heavy chalk line) is attached to the cable by means of a swivel.

Firing Procedure and Range The normal firing procedure for the AT Grenade M9A1 is followed. Extra care is taken that the trailing wire and cord are free of the grenade launcher and rifle, and that the trailing cord is carefully coiled on the ground, preferably to the right of the weapon. With the rifle at a 45° angle, the grapnel will attain a range of 75 to 100 yards.

COMMENT: This. method is one of many improvised techniques of clearing antipersonnel trip wire mines with grapnels. It is of limited application but would be useful as an aid in clearing mine fields to which covered approaches are available.

* * *

Hide Your AT Guns *Captain Don C. Wylie, Infantry Antitank Company,* ANZIO, ITALY: "Position security in this beachhead area is a real problem. The Germans held commanding observation and were quick to spot derelictions in concealment. On one occasion five out of six 57-mm antitank guns that were emplaced in a forward-battalion-position area were accurately located by the Germans either through improper camouflage or through movement near them during daylight. Just after dawn the enemy put down an. artillery concentration consisting of a mixture of impact and air-burst high explosive on each of these gun positions and put the entire crews of all five weapons out of action in not over 5 minutes.

"Five German tanks then moved in from the right flank on a road which ran just in front of the positions of the two front-line rifle companies. Without leaving the road, the tanks smothered the position of the right-company with fire, enabling accompanying German infantry to work down a ravine into the position, which was overwhelmed.

"The tanks then proceeded down the road to the position of the left company, losing one tank to the remaining AT gun, which they in turn destroyed. Again they smothered the company position with fire, while another German infantry unit overwhelmed it.

Visitors Not Desired "In this sector we allow no one to visit our forward AT gun positions during daylight nor are the gun crews allowed to move out from under the camouflage. Even at night we do not allow vehicles to approach the positions, thus insuring that their tracks will not disclose gun locations. Pedestrian traffic at night is restricted to well-defined trails or paths."

SOURCES

CHAPTER 1

U.S. War Department, FM 7-20, *Infantry Battalion* (Washington DC, U.S. Government Printing Office, October 1, 1944)

U.S. War Department, FM 7-5, *Organization and Tactics of Infantry: The Rifle Battalion* (Washington DC, U.S. Government Printing Office, October 1, 1940)

CHAPTER 2

U.S. War Department, FM 7-5, *Organization and Tactics of Infantry: The Rifle Battalion* (Washington DC, U.S. Government Printing Office, October 1, 1940)

U.S. War Department, FM 21-20, *Physical Training* (Washington DC, U.S. Government Printing Office, March 6, 1941)

U.S. Army, *Training Notes from Recent Fighting in Tunisia: Experiences, Observations & Opinions collected from Officers and Men of Front Line Units—March 18–30, 1943* (G-3 Training Section, AFHQ, 1943)

U.S. War Department, *Instructions for American Servicemen in Britain* (Washington DC, U.S. War Department, 1942)

U.S. War Department, *Short Guide to Iraq* (Washington DC, U.S. War Department, 1943)

CHAPTER 3

U.S. War Department, FM 7-5, *Organization and Tactics of Infantry: The Rifle Battalion* (Washington DC, U.S. Government Printing Office, October 1, 1940)

U.S. Army, FM 23-5, *U.S. Rifle, Caliber .30, M1* (Washington DC, HQ, Department of the Army, 1942)

U.S. War Department, FM 23-45, *Browning Machine Gun, Caliber .30 HB, M1919A4 Ground* (Washington DC, U.S. Government Printing Office, 1940)

U.S. War Department, *Weapon and Ammunition Technical Manual: Infantry Regiment, Parachute* (Washington DC, U.S. Government Printing Office, June 1944)

U.S. War Department, TM 9-294, *2.36-inch A.T. Rocket Launcher M1A1* (Washington DC, U.S. Government Printing Office, September 27, 1943)

CHAPTER 4

U.S. War Department, FM 7-10, *Rifle Company, Rifle Regiment* (Washington DC, U.S. Government Printing Office, June 2, 1942)

U.S. War Department, FM 7-5, *Organization and Tactics of Infantry: The Rifle Battalion* (Washington DC, U.S. Government Printing Office, October 1, 1940)

CHAPTER 5

U.S. War Department, *Combat Lessons No. 1: Rank and file in combat: What they're doing and how they do it* (Washington DC, U.S. Government Printing Office, 1944)

U.S. War Department, *Combat Lessons No. 4: Rank and file in combat: What they're doing and how they do it* (Washington DC, U.S. Government Printing Office, 1944)